Flow Blue

A COLLECTOR'S GUIDE TO PATTERNS, HISTORY, AND VALUES

JEFFREY B. SNYDER

REVISED & EXPANDED 4TH EDITION

Schiffer Publishing Ltd

4880 Lower Valley Road, Atglen, PA 19310 USA

Revised price guide: 2003
Copyright © 1999 & 2003 by Jeffrey B. Snyder
Library of Congress Control Number: 2002113321

ISBN: 0-7643-1720-2
Typeset in Zurich XCn BT/Aldine 721 BT
Printed in China
1 2 3 4

Published by Schiffer Publishing Ltd.
4880 Lower Valley Road
Atglen, PA 19310
Phone: (610) 593-1777; Fax: (610) 593-2002
E-mail: Schifferbk@aol.com
Please visit our web site catalog at
www.schifferbooks.com or write for a free catalog.
This book may be purchased from the publisher.
Please include $3.95 for shipping.

In Europe, Schiffer books are distributed by
Bushwood Books
6 Marksbury Ave.
Kew Gardens
Surrey TW9 4JF England
Phone: 44 (0)20-8392-8585; Fax: 44 (0)20-8392-9876
E-mail: Bushwd@aol.com
Free postage in the UK. Europe: air mail at cost

Please try your bookstore first. We are interested in hearing from authors with book ideas on related subjects.

Acknowledgments

I am very grateful to all the people who made this book possible. Dealers and collectors generously allowed me into their shops and homes, permitting me to disrupt their schedules and clutter their working and living spaces with a tangle of equipment. Others took the time to bring items to me at conventions. They all made the photographs in this book possible. Dealers and experts were also free with suggestions and insights which enriched the text. I would like to offer my thanks to each of these individuals: Marion Butz, The Antique Marketplace, Lancaster, Pennsylvania; Suzanne and William Hagenlocher; John and Nancy Harner, Dover Antique Mart, Smyrna, Delaware; Bonnie Hohl; Jacqueline Hunsicker; Arnold and Dorothy Kowalsky; William Leach; Louise and Charles Loehr, Louise's Old Things, Kutztown, Pennsylvania; Linda Machalski, L.G. Antiques, Hartley, Delaware; and Rosemary Wright. A special thanks to Arnold A. Kowalsky (908 North Broadway, Yonkers, NY 10701) for the price guide revisions and all of the information and friendly advice he has so generously provided over the past few years.

I would also like to thank Douglas Congdon-Martin, my editor, and the staff of Schiffer Publishing. Their professionalism and their help made this project easier.

Finally, I would like to thank my family. My wife Sherry, for reading my text and putting up with me during this project. My son, Michael, and daughter, Madeline, who keep me company at the computer when I write. Jim and Mary Alice Snyder, my parents, for their help with equipment and for their love and enthusiasm.

Contents

Dedication

This book is dedicated to my family and close friends, who have always encouraged me to write.

Thanks

The attributes which define Flow Blue are all present in this Manilla pattern plate, dating from 1845. *Courtesy of Louise and Charles Loehr, Louise's Old Things, Kutztown, Pennsylvania.* $65-105

Introduction

It is truly amazing that anything produced within the last three hundred years has survived to be collected. Nine-tenths of all man-made objects produced in that time have been destroyed. Only when an object has survived long enough to be recognized as old, and therefore valuable, do the odds against it improve.[1] That, of course, is what makes collecting anything such a rewarding challenge. The challenge is heightened in the case of mass produced materials. These objects were used hard and used often. After all, if they were broken, they were replicable. They were not unique. Therefore, collecting Flow Blue ceramics, mass produced and regularly used as they were, is a challenge for anyone who has ever been entranced by their rich color or softly flowing designs.

This book was written to aid in the identification of these alluring wares and to provide insights into Flow Blue's development and evolution through time. Collectors, armed with the knowledge of how the objects of their desire were manufactured and used, will understand their acquisition's place in the past and will be able to distinguish between original Flow Blue ceramics, their closely related but unknown transfer printed cousins, and modern reproductions.

Only ten percent of all man-made objects produced in the last 300 years have survived. *The author's collection.* $25-50

The subject is approached from my perspective as an historical archaeologist. It is organized to provide sufficient background history and identifiable traits to allow you to enter a dealer's shop or arrive at an estate sale ready to identify and purchase, with confidence, the pieces you want to collect, from your period of interest. Read this book carefully and you will be able to identify the general types of Flow Blue, understand the significance of the pieces in the lives of the people who used them, date the pieces you see by their identifying characteristics, and learn enough history to know when you are looking at the real thing.

What is Flow Blue?

The first step in understanding Flow Blue is to define the ware. The term Flow Blue describes ceramic wares decorated with transfer printed designs, usually printed in dark cobalt blue ink, which have been caused to bleed into the undecorated portions of the vessels, creating a blurred image. The cobalt blue bleeds or "flows" over the white body when the glaze applied over the decoration is fired in the kiln.[2] The result has been described by some as fuzzy, ugly...a virtual potting faux pas. But if you are reading this book, you know better.

Flow Blue ceramics came in many forms, from lowly chamber pots to lofty tea services and tablewares. By some estimates Flow Blue was produced in as many as 1500 patterns as well.[3] While many of the patterns were printed in a deep cobalt blue, the shades and colors did vary in some cases. Some patterns are very blurred, or "flown", while others have only the faintest light blue halo around the edges of the pattern, making them virtually indistinguishable from unknown transfer prints. For the new collector of Flow Blue, all these variations may be confusing. Even seasoned veterans can find the identification of little known and barely flown patterns daunting.

Where Was Flow Blue Produced and Sold?

England was the first nation to produce Flow Blue ceramics. By the late eighteenth century, English potters were the dominant force in the market of mass produced pottery. It is no surprise they were the largest producers of Flow Blue wares. English potters also continued to produce Flow Blue throughout the nineteenth and into the twentieth century. Other European potters joined the English tide later in the nineteenth century. Several American potteries produced their own Flow Blue wares near the end of the nineteenth century.[4]

Chamber pot decorated in the Perth pattern dating from circa 1891-1914. *Courtesy of Louise and Charles Loehr, Louise's Old Things, Kutztown, Pennsylvania.* $150+

Only the faintest blue halo from the flowing process is visible on this Pekin pattern plate dating from 1845. *Courtesy of Louise and Charles Loehr, Louise's Old Things, Kutztown, Pennsylvania.* $75-150

Heavily flown Pelew pattern teapot, circa 1842-1867. *Courtesy of Jacqueline Hunsicker.* $800+

Date Ranges & Popularity

The production of Flow Blue ceramics nearly coincides with the reign of Queen Victoria, after whom the Victorian Age was named, who ruled England from 1837 to 1901. While there are modern examples, Flow Blue ceramics were primarily manufactured from 1825 through the early 1900s. During the first decade of production, Flow Blue wares were few. The pieces made were not widely produced or disseminated. After 1835 mass production of Flow Blue began and the wares became very popular. As some of the first mass produced decorative designs on ceramic wares (along with the unflown transfer printed wares) they were much in demand. During the mid-nineteenth century plain white ironstone rose in popularity and vied with al the transfer prints. By the early twentieth century, the popular era of Flow Blue ceramics had passed. [5] However, today Flow Blue ceramics enjoy a resurgence in demand among avid collectors with a taste for Victorian design or history.

The study and collection of Flow Blue ceramics is a fascinating and enjoyable pastime. I hope this book will clear up any confusion you may feel concerning the staggering variety of Flow Blue wares available and will help you get the greatest possible enjoyment out of your search for Flow Blue.

Footnotes

[1] Ivor Noël Hume, All the Best Rubbish, (New York: Harper & Row, Publishers, 1974), 166.

[2] Mary Frank Gaston, The Collector's Encyclopedia of Flow Blue China, (Paducah, Kentucky: Collector's Books, 1983), 7.

[3] "Flow Blue China," Treasure Chest, December, 1991.

[4] James Deetz, In Small Things Forgotten, (Garden City, New York: Anchor press/Doubleday, 1977), 58; and Gaston, The Collector's Encyclopedia of Flow Blue China, 7.

[5] Petra Williams, Flow Blue China. An Aid to Identification, (Jeffersontown, Kentucky: Fountain House East, 1971), 7.

A portion of a tea service in the Kirkee pattern including (left to right) a sugar bowl, teapot and cream pitcher with 8 panel sides. The three date from circa 1861. *Courtesy of Jacqueline Hunsicker.* $1500+

Chapter 1
History

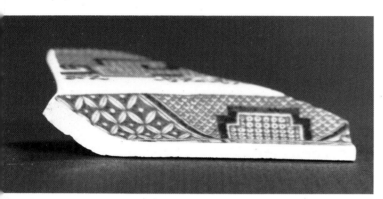

Cross section of an earthenware plate decorated with a transfer printed oriental pattern. *The author's collection.*

Earthenware decorated with flowing blue transfer prints embody much that defined the tastes and ideals of the nineteenth century Victorian Age. Understanding Flow Blue's past and what the pieces represented in their day provides the collector with a window into the Victorian mind.

Their earthenware body paste was the culmination of the eighteenth century search for a strong and durable ceramic which could survive the rough journeys to foreign markets in Europe and America while presenting a bright surface rivaling Chinese porcelain in its whiteness. The success of an earlier strong body material propelled the British potters into world dominance of the ceramic market and the body paste of Flow Blue ceramics continued the British potters' rise.

The printed design borne on its surface marked an early success in English mass production, transfer printing, which allowed patterns to be cheaply, quickly and uniformly applied to a large and growing ceramic stock. The patterns themselves were designed to appeal to a newly accessible mass market from roughly 1830 tot he early 1900s.[1] The variety in dining services shipped to America mark a significant change in American eating habits and their views of privacy as well.[2] All of this embodied in Flow Blue ceramics.

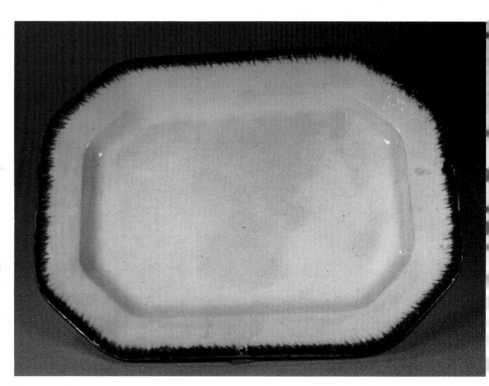

Pearlware platter decorated with a blue shell-edge rim. *Courtesy of Linda Machalski, L. G. Antiques, Hartley, Delaware.*

Origins of Earthenware

The production of earthenware pottery was a time honored tradition among English potters centuries before Flow Blue. Earthenwares are potteries with soft, water-absorbent bodies made impermeable by glazing. Glazes consist of lead sulfides with additives introduced to add color or opacity to an otherwise colorless and transparent substance. Earthenwares, as opposed to stonewares and porcelain, were the predominant body types to which Flow Blue decorations were applied. Earthenware is opaque and will not allow light to pass through it. Hold your hand up behind it and you will not see its shadow through the pottery. Porcelain, on the other hand, is translucent, allowing light to pas through it.[3]

Cream & Pearlware

During the second half of the eighteenth century, English potters, particularly those of the Staffordshire district, refined their wares. Earthenwares became thinner and harder, and the body color was lightened to nearly that of the coveted Chinese porcelain's white. After 1750 these improvements led to creamware, a thin, hard-fired, cream colored earthenware dipped in a clear glaze. Josiah Wedgwood may have perfected creamware in 1762.[4] From 1765 to the early 1770s Josiah Wedgwood experimented with the potting of a ware whiter than creamware which he christened "Pearl White" (pearlware) in 1779. Wedgwood decided not to produce "Pearl White" in quantity because he was financially bound to his creamware. Other potters, however, were not so restricted and by 1787 there were at least eight factories producing pearlware in Burslem alone. Pearlware was used for everything from dining services to chamber pots; however, it appeared most frequently in the form of shell-edged plates with rims painted either blue or green.[5]

Ironstone

By 1820, pearlware was on its way out, being replaced by various forms of hard white wares and semi-porcelains which had evolved out of it. White wares had a harder and whiter paste than pearlware and a clearer colorless glaze unavailable in pearlware. These ran parallel to the "stone china" produced by Spode in 1805 and Charles James Mason's famous "Ironstone China" patented in the Staffordshire Potteries in July of 1813. "Mason's Patent Ironstone China" was the best attempt to perfect a new and inexpensive but durable earthenware body during the early nineteenth century. The name alone conveyed a sense of strength associated in the public mind with china. Mason's Ironstone was an improvement on white ware with a harder body and a thinner and finer profile than other wares called ironstone. A small amount of cobalt blue was introduced into the glaze to make ironstone appear whiter than it would if its body paste were left exposed beneath a clear glaze. This process often left a pale blue puddling in crevices around handles and along the interior edges of foot rings.[6]

Ironstone's sturdy body was often used for dinner and dessert services and was adorned with designs mimicking the Oriental style. Most Flow Blue designs were applied to Iron-

Note the light blue puddling of the glaze around the inner edge of the foot ring characteristic of ironstone. *Courtesy of Louise and Charles Loehr, Louise's Old Things, Kutztown, Pennsylvania.*

Early English designs mimicked Oriental styles. This Beauties Of China plate design dates from 1845. *Courtesy of Louise and Charles Loehr, Louise's Old Things, Kutztown, Pennsylvania.* $75-150+

stone. While the early potting and decorative standards were not perfect, the unusual new ware was able to compete well with most expensive porcelains. So successful was Mason's Patent Ironstone China that practically every potter of the period from 1830 through 1880 made versions of it.

The most accurate way of identifying ironstone is from the manufacturer's mark which appear on the back of flat wares and on the bottom of hollow forms of most ironstone beginning in the mid-nineteenth century. However, ironstone has been called many things by various manufacturers in an attempt to lure the consumer to their particular ware by making it seem special or unique. Some of the creative names applied to ironstone include "Granite China," "Opaque China," "Stone China," and "Stone ware," among others.[7] These and other appellations may be found among the photographs of the manufacturers' marks in Chapters 5 and 6.

Until the late 1840s ironstone was usually decorated with transfer prints, as in Flow Blue, or with painted shell edged rims. During the 1850s plain, undecorated ironstone became popular and in the decades after the Civil War undecorated wares were widely produced in both England and the United States.[8]

At its best Mason's Ironstone closely rivaled porcelain, but for everyday use it had the upper hand. It was used for everything from table and tea services to toilet wares during the nineteenth century. Pearlware, whiteware and porcelain were commonly used as well. What distinguished between them most in the Victorian mind was not so much the ware type as the decorations on them.[9]

Rise of the British Potters

Creamware launched England's conquest of the world tableware market. So successful were the English potters that

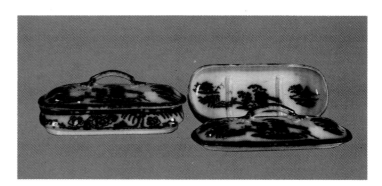

Toilet wares in ironstone included these tooth brush holders dating from circa 1845. *Coutesy of Bonne Hohl.* $600+

Dorothy luncheon set (one place setting and tea service), in ironstone. *Courtesy of Jacqueline Hunsicker.* $800-1000 set
(see page 97)

American colonial government's instituted aggressive "Buy American" plans, but to no avail. Politicians and consumers have not really changed much. With the exception of a few coarse red wares—the stuff of storage jugs and milk pans—English pottery dominated the American market. American potters simply could not compete with the Staffordshire potteries. Ironstone helped perpetuate England's hold on the market. The demand for ironstone wares quickly developed after its introduction. Mass produced transfer printed designs decorated much of the ironstone produced, meeting the demand for new and colorful wares at a lower price than porcelain. Among them, beginning in earnest in the 1840s, were Flow Blue decorated wares.[10]

Origins of Transfer Printing

Complementing the development of durable and popular ceramic wares was the creation of the first mass produced decorations on ceramics, the transfer prints. Transfer printing allowed a potter to quickly duplicate a pattern by transferring it from a copper plate to ceramic vessels via a specially treated paper. Transfer printing was much quicker and cheaper than the handpainting techniques used prior to its introduction. The process also allowed people to buy complete sets of dishes that were virtually identical, a feat never before possible with the handpainted wares.

While Janssen, Delamain and Brooks, at York House, Battersea, probably produced the earliest transfer prints in red and purple, Sadler and Green of Liverpool are recognized for perfecting the technique in 1756. Sadler and Green produced black prints on delftware, a very soft bodied ware, and creamware. The early transfer prints were applied over top of the glaze. The "overglazed" patterns quickly showed signs of wear when used. Printing in underglaze blue on earthenwares would not become popular until the end of the eighteenth century.[11]

Once transfer printing was accepted by potters as a decorative technique, it quickly gained popularity with the public. The earliest patterns copied Chinese designs. The earliest transfer printed "chinoiseries" including the "willow pattern" were printed on pearlware. The "willow" motif was invented by Thomas Minton at Caughley and shipped to China for use on Chinese export porcelain. The first fruits of this round trip journey arrived back in England in 1792.[12]

Early in the nineteenth century some potters broke from the near obsession for copying Chinese designs colored in a deep cobalt blue. Cobalt blue was discovered to be the only color early on that would survive the high firing temperatures necessary for underglazing the design. Completely new designs came into fashion. Wide borders, normally floral, became popular, and many manufacturers began catering to American markets with the engraving of exotic foreign views or the arms of American states. Print quality improved as the engravers learned to use dots instead of lines to create their patterns. However, the overall quality of the art work varied according to the resources of the potter and the wherewithal of his customers. The leading firms produced beautiful ceramics and finely engraved transfer printed patterns. Lesser firms produced simpler designs reflective of their assets.[13]

Origins of Flow Blue

In the 1820s it was discovered that although the cobalt blue used in transfer printing would blur naturally, it could also be induced to flow. The results were pleasing to the eye and pleasing to the potters. The flowing color hid a myriad of potting mistakes. Some of the pieces were so heavily flown that it was impossible to identify either the center or border patterns. As time passed and underglazing techniques improved, other colors were used to make flowing wares including puce, mulberry, and sepia, but blue was by far the most popular.[14]

American Cultural Change

Paralleling the developments in the British potting industry were changes in American colonial culture as it headed into the nineteenth century which accelerated the demand for British wares. By the early 1800s, families began acquiring chairs and dining utensils among other things. They were able to make mealtimes more important social occasions. Most white Americans began looking forward to eating individual servings at a table set with personal knives, forks, glasses, bowls and plates—preferably matching ones. This had not been the practice of the eighteenth century, where resources were often severely limited and dining was a largely communal affair with wooden serving bowls and shared cooking pots. Anything that resembled that old communal way of dining in the early nineteenth century was increasingly likely to be viewed with distaste. In its place developed an emphasis on symmetry, balance and a greater awareness of the individual. This theme echoes throughout every aspect of the Victorian Age.[15]

Historic records illustrate the change. By the 1770s full

The "willow" motif, invented by Thomas Minton at Caughley, England. *Courtesy of Louise and Charles Loehr, Louise's Old Things, Kutztown, Pennsylvania.* $75-95

Transfer printing allowed consumers to own complete sets of virtually identical table wares for the first time. *Courtesy of Linda Machalski, L. G. Antiques, Hartley, Delaware.* $2500+ (service for eight)

English potters catered to the American market with exotic views of faraway lands as in the scene on this tooth brush holder. *Courtesy of Louise and Charles Loehr, Louise's Old Things, Kutztown, Pennsylvania.* $100-300

sets of dishes appear in households. In the 1780s, complete services appear. By the early 1800s these services were becoming par for the course. The American consumer was eager to receive England's mass produced wares and put the past behind them. English potters were well-prepared to meet the demand. Meanwhile, American potters would fight hard to carve out a niche in the overwhelmingly British market.[16]

American Manufacturers

Pottery making in the British American colonies began around 1625 and by the 1650s many of the colonists' simple communal ceramic needs were satisfied by local craftsmen. However, American potters produced wares vastly inferior to imported English wares until well into the eighteenth century. The early American potters wares found no markets beyond their local areas where they had the advantages of lower prices and constant availability.[17]

By the reign of Queen Victoria, American factories were turning out ceramics at a steady pace. At first, the American potters copied the British wares in much the same way the British had copied the Chinese, even to the point of copying the British coat of arms as a back mark.[18] The British ceramics were considered by American families to be the very best and American potters wanted their wares to compare closely with the British competition in every way possible. If some American consumers were actually fooled into thinking they were getting the real thing, so much the better.

The American prejudice towards British wares ran deep and was slow to disappear. A number of American companies produced Flow Blue in an attempt to penetrate the market and break England's hold on the hearts, minds and pocketbooks of their countrymen. Three companies whose wares are commonly found today from among the many who produced services and toilet sets are Mercer Pottery (1868-circa 1937) in Trenton, New Jersey, Wheeling Pottery Company (1879-circa 1910) in Wheeling, West Virginia, and Burgess and Campbell (1860-1940) in Trenton, New Jersey. They were grudgingly accepted by American consumers.[19]

Historical Value of Flow Blue

Many have expressed the opinion that Flow Blue ceramics were a "poor mans china." History, the variety of table service pieces found in Flow Blue, and potters' price lists tell a different story, at least through the middle of the nineteenth century. History and common sense tell us that people of different social classes followed different eating habits. The wealthier the household, the greater the varieties of foods they

Mercer Pottery produced this Luzerne soup bowl in circa 1902. *Courtesy of Louise and Charles Loehr, Louise's Old Things, Kutztown, Pennsylvania.* $40-75

consumed and the greater the variety (and the higher the cost) of the table services they ate it from. Flow Blue dinner and luncheon services came in an almost mind boggling array of forms and functions. It is not likely that a family of modest means and simple diet would have had much use for this broad spectrum of table services.

Potters' price fixing lists, by which manufacturers controlled the costs of their products, also suggest that Flow Blue wares were not an every day purchase. The Staffordshire potters had a series of price fixing agreements in the eighteenth and nineteenth centuries. Some of these lists have survived and are available for several years between 1770 and 1855. These price lists provide cost information for the various sizes of vessels based on their decoration.[20] They reveal the comparative value the potters placed on their products.

In the 1790s, transfer printed vessels were 3 to 5 times more expensive than undecorated vessels. All of the transfer printed wares, even early willow patterns which were the cheapest of the transfer printed patterns, were only less expensive to purchase than porcelain. Until at least the late 1850s, Flow Blue patterns were priced even higher than regular transfer printed patterns. Most North American archaeological sites dating to the first half of the nineteenth century contain few ceramics that exceed transfer printed wares in terms of cost or social status and Flow Blue wares are among them.[21]

In 1855 Flow Blue plates are listed at prices significantly above the price of transfer printed plates in Robert Heron's price list. Compared with other transfer prints, Flow Blue remained a relatively expensive ware, despite the change in consumer tastes. As the century progressed, transfer printed wares became cheaper and their consumption greatly increased. Although the demand for printed wares increased again in the 1870s, the period when Japanese styles were introduced, a wider variety of wares became available to a wider range of consumers by the late nineteenth century. Some late patterns remain aimed at high income consumers while others are obviously targeted towards people of more modest means.[22] Of course, today the collector will find that the prices for some of the most sought after and rare pieces are far above anything the Staffordshire potters ever dreamed of when they were creating their price fixing lists.

Footnotes

[1] George L. Miller, "Classification and Economic Sealing of Nineteenth Century Ceramics," (Historical Archaeology 14:1, 1980), 2.

[2] James Deetz, In Small Things Forgotten, (Garden City, New York: Anchor Press/Doubleday, 1977), 48-50.

[3] Petra Williams, Flow Blue China. An Aid to Identification, (Jeffersontown, Kentucky: Fountain House East, 1971), 3.

[4] Deetz, In Small Things Forgotten, 47; and Ivor Noël Hume, A Guide to Artifacts of Colonial America, (New York; Alfred A. Knopf, 1969), 123-124.

[5] Noël Hume, A Guide to Artifacts of Colonial America, 128-131.

[6] ibid, 130-131; and Geoffrey A. Godden, British Porcelain. An Illustrated Guide, (New York: Clarkson N. Potter, Inc./Publisher, 1974), 204.

[7] Godden, British Porcelain. An Illustrated Guide, 204.

[8] Godden, British Porcelain. An Illustrated Guide, 204.

[9] Miller, "Classification and Economic Scaling of Nineteenth Century Ceramics," 2.

[10] Deetz, In Small Things Forgotten, 58.

[11] Noël Hume, A Guide to Artifacts of Colonial America, 128-129.

[12] ibid, 129.

[13] Godden, British Porcelain. An Illustrated Guide, 229.

[14] Williams, Flow Blue China. An Aid to Identification, 5.

[15] Jack Larkin, The Reshaping of Everyday Life, 1790-1840, (New York: Harper and Row, Publishers, 1988), 180.

[16] Williams, Flow Blue China. An Aid to Identification, 58-60; and Larkin, The Reshaping of Everyday Life, 1790-1840, 180-182.

[17] Noël Hume, A Guide to Artifacts of Colonial America, 98-99

[18] Williams, Flow Blue China. An Aid to Identification, 6.

[19] ibid, 6.

[20] Miller, "Classification and Economic Scaling of Nineteenth Century Ceramics," 3-4; and George L. Miller " Revised Set of CC Index Values for Classification and Economic Scaling of English Ceramics from 1787 to 1880," (Historical Archaeology 25:1, 1991), 9.

[21] ibid, 3-4.

[22] Deetz, In Small Things Forgotten, 51; Miller, "Classification and Economic Scaling of Nineteenth Century Ceramics," 28-29; and Miller "A Revised Set of CC Index Values for Classification and Economic Scaling of English Ceramics from 1787 to 1880," 9.

Chapter 2
Transfer Printing and Flow Blue

Knowing how a thing was created always provides insights into what to look for when collecting any object. Understanding the process involved in creating Flow Blue wares will help in its identification.

Artisans Involved

The 1500 or so transfer printed patterns found on Flow Blue ceramics were created by artisans, some greatly skilled and others not so capable. Only the largest and wealthiest firms could hire their own artist engravers. Smaller companies were supplied with their patterns by engraving firms. The artists who engraved the copper plates necessary for transfer printing occasionally became famous. A design of theirs would take off and as a result be copied in many forms with many variations on the theme by other potters. A few, such as Thomas Minton's Willow pattern, are still in use today.[1]

Willow pedestal bowl. *Courtesy of Louise and Charles Loehr, Louise's Old Things, Kutztown, Pennsylvania.* $700+

Production of Transfer Prints

While few artisan engravers became famous, transfer printing became a renowned and powerful mass production tool. It allowed a potter to reproduce many copies of the same pattern quickly with the aid of only semi-skilled laborers, and without the expense of employing trained artists. The majority of Flow Blue ceramics are solely decorated with underglaze designs, which had an advantage over overglazed patterns because the underglazed pattern was sealed and could not wear off through time and use.

To create any transfer prints, first engravers designed or adapted a suitable pattern to the shape of the pieces to be decorated. The pattern was then transferred to a flat sheet of copper by cutting or etching lines or dots into the copper. The deeper or thicker the line or dot, or the closer these were placed together, the darker would be the color. When the engraving was completed there was one copper plate for each size or shape of ceramic to be decorated. Then that particular pattern was ready for use. At this point the copper plate was warmed to prepare it for the application of the pigment.[2]

Once heated, the plate was ready for the application of a thick oily ceramic pigment, normally cobalt blue. The blue pigment color was obtained from the mineral cobalt. Cobalt blue was the one color the Chinese discovered would tolerate high temperatures required to fire a glaze on a ceramic body. The popularity for this underglaze blue pigment was established by the imported Chinese porcelains, most of which were painted solely in cobalt blue. From about the 1780s potters producing earthenwares sought to copy the Chinese with the help of underglaze cobalt blue prints. The ceramic pigment was rubbed into the recessed design, excess pigment was removed from the plate with a palette knife, and the surface of the copper plate was then rubbed clean. Only the recessed engraved design remained filled with pigment and the plate was now considered "charged" and ready for use.[3]

At this point a special tissue-like transfer paper was applied to the heated and charged copper plate, and both were placed under an even pressure. The pressure transferred the

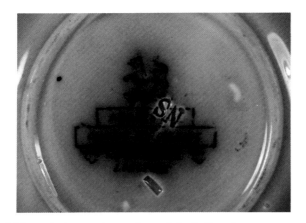

A fairly typical manufacturer's mark including the pattern name, name of the manufacturer, and the town where the factory was located. This mark was produced by T.J. & J. Mayer, Longport, Staffordshire, England, including the Arabesque pattern name, ca. 1843 to the mid-1850s. *Courtesy of Louise and Charles Loehr, Louise's Old Things, Kutztown, Pennsylvania.*

pigment to the paper, which was then lifted from the copper plate and passed to a woman who cut away the excess paper.[4]

Once the paper was ready, a woman then carefully positioned the cut and charged paper onto an unglazed plate or other object and rubbed it down with soft-soap flannels. These women were responsible for placing the pattern correctly, for joining the seams of the borders and designs, and for applying the manufacturer's mark or back stamp. The manufacturer's mark usually gives the pattern name and initials or name of the maker and in many cases the town where the factory is located. Once transferred to the paper the mark was cut off and applied to the backs of plates or to the base of hollow wares. Sometimes the mark was omitted and we get unmarked pieces.[5]

While these marks are one of your best and easiest clues in identifying a piece, a few of them will always remain a mystery. There were so many manufacturers, producing such enormous quantities of wares that not all the marks may be identified. Also, some potters stayed in business for such a short time and made so few pieces that the identity of their marks has been lost to history. There is an additional problem for Flow Blue collectors. When the pattern was flown as described below, the manufacturer's mark flowed with it and some of the marks became illegible.

Once the transfer paper was applied to the piece, the paper was then soaked off and normally the object was then lightly fired to burn out the oil in the pigment. After the oil was burned off, the object was dipped in glaze and fired at a high heat so that the blue design becomes an underglaze print. Occasionally Flow Blue wares exhibit overglazed patterns supplementing the underglazed blue design.[6] Overglazed prints were applied to previously glazed objects using methods similar to those described above but with inks that were more heat sensitive.

Transfer printed designs were used only when a relatively long run of a particular design was required. No one went to the expense of engraving a copper plate for a single object or even a small run and no one ever engraved a costly set of coppers for a service, if only a few were to be made. With these restrictions it is easy to see that no printed design was ever unique. There were no one of a kind issues in transfer printing, flown or unflown.[7]

Flowing of the Print

In the 1820s, printers discovered that although cobalt blue would blur naturally, it could be made to flow by introducing lime or chloride of ammonia during the glaze firing. The ink spread to create a softer print with smoother lines and a deeper color than was possible with unaltered transfer prints. There were additional benefits to the flown design as well. The deep blurring covered printing faults and stilt marks and served to hide a variety of other defects such as glaze bubbles.

Idiosyncrasies

While transfer printing and Flow Blue are examples of early mass production, it is worth remembering that the patterns were applied to wares by hand. Individuals placed them and the results were not perfect. It is interesting to search for signs of individuality when looking for Flow Blue ceramics. Here are some of the imperfections to look for.

When matching transfer paper to wares, individual sections were cut out and fit to the wares. On lightly flown pieces, the match lines are often visible. More interesting is what happens to transfer printed wares containing inscriptions.

Lightly flown Abbey print revealing an unhidden match line. *The author's collection.*

Another example of obvious match lines that the flowing process was meant to hide on a Lobelia platter. *Courtesy of John and Nancy Harner, Dover Antique Mart, Smyrna, Delaware.*

Transfer printing was also a messy job. The ink did get on the hands of the women transferring the designs to the wares. From time to time you may discover a finger or thumb print on the back of a plate from the original transferor. This is the only truly unique pattern you will ever find on transfer printed wares. If there are no finger prints, on earlier wares there may be stilt marks.

Stilt marks consist of three small dots in the glaze made by triangular spur pieces which separated the plates in the early nineteenth century kilns. Later in the nineteenth century different measures were taken to separate the plates and the stilt marks disappeared.[9]

Three stilt marks are visible inside the foot ring. *Courtesy of Louise and Charles Loehr, Louise's Old Things, Kutztown, Pennsylvania.*

While there are not many of these in Flow Blue, there are a few.

Hastily engraved copper plates provided transfers that had to be cut and trimmed to fit vessels of different sizes. The trimming and fitting process often led to nearly illegible inscriptions as letters were cropped off here and there. Pictures remained whole but words suffered, not that it mattered to the women fitting the pattern. Few of them could read.[8]

Quick Changes

Trying to memorize all the Flow Blue patterns and their names would surely drive you crazy, not only because there are so many designs but because it was so easy to transform one design into another. Several ways in which this was done include simply changing the pattern name itself on the manufacturer's mark or, if the potter were more ambitious, by omitting either the rim or the center design and giving the altered pattern the new name. There were other ways to add the confusion as well.

An unaltered portion of the Hong Kong center pattern was printed on this small cup plate. The cup plate measures 4 1/8" in diameter. *Courtesy of Bonne Hohl.* $100-150

With a little creative cutting, the same Hong Kong pattern could be quickly altered into patterns with very different appearances and a different name as well. On these two cup plates a small portion of the Hong Kong center design was used on each with a floral border to create the new look. The cup plates measure 4 1/8" in diameter. *Courtesy of Bonne Hohl.* $100-150 ea.

Many manufacturers purchased their designs from firms which specialized in designing printed patterns, and engraved the copper plates necessary for printing. A popular design would be sold to several firms and the same mark design would be used, but a different purchaser's initials would be engraved on it. Or a pattern may be sold to twenty different firms and each may chose a different name for the same design. Duplication also occurred when a factory went bankrupt and was sold. The copper plates purchased in the deal carried the manufacturer's mark of the bankrupt factory formerly producing the ware. The buyer would use the same name and pattern but would add his own factory mark to the pre-existing one.[10]

Footnotes
[1] Petra Williams, Flow Blue China. An Aid to Identification, (Jeffersontown, Kentucky; Fountain House East, 1971), 4.
[2] Geoffrey A Godden, British Porcelain. An Illustrated Guide, (New York: Clarkson N. Potter, Inc./Publisher, 1974), 228-230.
[3] ibid, 228-230.
[4] ibid, 228-230
[5] ibid, 228-230.
[6] ibid, 228-230.
[7] ibid, 228-230.
[8] Ivor Noël Hume, All the Best Rubbish, (New York: Harper and Row, Publishers, 1974), 154.
[9] Williams, Flow Blue China. An Aid to Identification, 5.
[10] ibid, 4.

Chapter 3
Victorian Flow

Many new collectors find themselves staggered by the multitude of vessel forms and shapes used during the Victorian Age. To simplify the matter, I have broken the types down into three general classes, dinner wares, tea services, and everything else.

Dinner Wares

American Need for a Changing Service

As we have seen, by the early 1800s the demand for a diversified dining service was building in America as the American mind set changed from communal to individual. Everyone wanted their own place setting. Potters were quick to accommodate the demand with a wide variety of specialized wares.

Dinner Service Components

Dining services (including all meals) were composed of the following wares[1]

Many of these dining or serving pieces are portrayed in the photographs which follow. The vast majority of the pieces are descriptively named and require no further explanation.

Shapes among the dining services changed through time. Prior to the middle of the nineteenth century, Flow Blue plates and bowls are found to have predominantly paneled plate edges and bowl rims. During the middle of the century, these paneled edges are gradually replaced with rounded and scalloped edges. By the last quarter of the nineteenth century, paneled edges are out of fashion and the round and scalloped edges are common. Additionally, during the first half of the last century, handles and knobs or finials on vessel lids are ornate and many hollow forms have pedestal bases. By the late nineteenth century these ornate treatments have been replaced by simpler lines and there are fewer pedestal pieces.

Bone dishes	Butter dishes	Butter pats
Cereal dishes	Cheese dishes	Chocolate cups
Chocolate pots	Chop plates	Coffee cups
Compotes	Covered butter dishes with drainers	Covered casseroles
		Egg Cups
Covered vegetable dishes	Dinner plates	Gravy boats with trays
Flat soups	Footed custard cups with handles	Mugs
Individual oval vegetables	Ladles	Pickle dishes
Nappies	Oval setting dishes	Pitchers, 1 pt., 1 qt., 2 qt.
Pickle dishes	Pie plates	Punch cups
Platters	Potato or berry bowls	Sauce boats
Round serving dishes	Salt dishes	Soup tureens with trays
Sauce tureens with stands	Soup plates with flange rims	
Spoon trays		

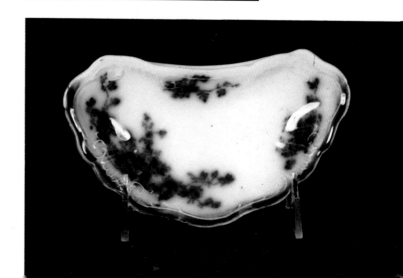

Marechal Niel Bone Dish dating to circa 1891-1914 and produced by W.H. Grindley & Company. *Courtesy of John and Nancy Harner, Dover Antique Mart, Smyrna, Delaware.* $75+

Covered Vegetable Dish in the Hong Kong pattern dated to circa 1845 and produced by Charles Meigh. This is a rare and elegant piece measuring 6" tall x 8 1/8" in diameter. *Courtesy of Bonne Hohl.* $800+

Platter in the Kyber pattern from circa 1870, by John Meir & Sons. This platter measures 18" x 14". *Courtesy of Louise and Charles Loehr, Louise's Old Things, Kutztown, Pennsylvania.* $600-700

Tea Services and Variations In Form Through Time

Tea Service Composition

Tea services were composed of the following items[2]:

Cake plates	Creamers	Cup plates
Cups (handleless first, handled cups and saucers later)	Milk pitcher	Sugar bowl
Tea plates	Tea pot	

Tea Service Introduction and Form

The introduction of tea from the East produced a new social phenomenon among the upper class, the "tea ceremony," and with it a demand for new ceramic wares. English potters quickly copied the Chinese fashion and produced handleless tea cups and large bowl-like saucers. The Chinese used handleless cups because they poured tea into their saucer and drank from that as the tea cooled.[3] The British followed the form by producing handleless cups for their markets. Examples of handleless cups manufactured by British potters may be found until approximately the last quarter of the nineteenth century.

Cup plates were invented as a convenient place to rest the cup while the tea in the saucer cooled. Between roughly 1765 and 1850, British cup plates were always made of earthenware. After 1850 they were made of glass. In America, glass cup plates were introduced in 1825. Early cup plates were about four inches in diameter. After 1825, their size gradually diminished. Few cup plates were marked.[4]

Sugar bowls were very large until the middle 1860s. Prior to the mid-1860s sugar was processed in conical molds. These molds created a large cone shaped sugar "loaf" weighing approximately five pounds. Sugar nippers were used to cut off pieces of the loaf to be placed in the large, widemouthed sugar bowls. Sugar tongs were then used on the table to lift the lumps from bowl to cup. After the mid-1860s, the process of granulating sugar crystals was developed, ended the need for large sugar bowls.[5]

English handleless tea cup and large saucer in the Chinese fashion. Hindustan pattern dating from circa 1855. The cup measures 2 5/8" tall and 4" in diameter. The saucer measures 6" in diameter. *Courtesy of Louise and Charles Loehr, Louise's Old Things, Kutztown, Pennsylvania.* $150

Before 1860 sugar bowls were much larger than today. Sugar was processed in large loaves and broken into pieces. A large, widemouthed bowl was needed. This is an Indian pattern sugar bowl dating from circa 1840 and measuring 8" tall and 5" in diameter at the mouth. *Courtesy of Louise and Charles Loehr, Louise's Old Things, Kutztown, Pennsylvania.* $300-450

English cup plate used to set a tea cup on while tea cooled in the saucer. It is adorned with the Columbia pattern dating from circa 1846 and measures 4" in diameter. *Courtesy of Louise and Charles Loehr, Louise's Old Things, Kutztown, Pennsylvania.* $100+

Other Materials
Other Victorian wares produced in Flow Blue include[6]

Baskets for Egg Cups	Biscuit jars	Bureau trays
Candlesticks	Chamber pots	Chargers
Egg Drainers	Ewers	Hat pin holders
Hot water plates	Jardinières	Picture plates
Pin trays	Shaving mugs	Soap dishes
Tiles	Toothbrush holders	Toy sets of dishes
Toy tea sets	Vases and Wall pocket vases	Wash pitchers and basins
		Waste bowl

Aubrey pattern chamber pot dating from 1903, produced by Doulton & Company, and measuring 5 1/2" tall and 9 1/4" in diameter. *Courtesy of Louise and Charles Loehr, Louise's Old Things, Kutztown, Pennsylvania.* $1500+ set

Shaving mug adorned with the Hong Kong pattern dating from circa 1845, produced by Charles Meigh, and measuring 2 7/8" tall and 2 3/4" in diameter. Courtesy of Bonne Hohl. $500-650

Oban pattern wash pitcher and basin dating from circa 1900, produced by Myott, Sons & Company. The pitcher measures 18" x 12" x 5" and the basin measures 12" in diameter. This is a rare piece. The pattern is very uncommon. *Courtesy of Linda Machalski, L.G. Antiques, Hartley, Delaware.* $500-650

Dating Techniques for Flow Blue Patterns

The following dating guidelines will allow you to quickly recognize certain characteristics which will help identify Flow Blue ceramics and determine their period of manufacture.

In Chapter 5, the wares have been organized into three general periods. The pattern designs change over the years and general guidelines may be followed in identifying the period of most pieces. There are exceptions such as occur in wares produced during transition periods, of course, but these guidelines generally work quite well.

The three periods are:
Early Victorian: c. 1835-1860
Middle Victorian: 1860s-1870s
Late Victorian: 1880s-the early 1900s (We will use the first quarter of the twentieth century to define the early 1900s)

The patterns used during these three periods may be categorized generally as:
Early Victorian: Oriental and Scenic Patterns
Middle Victorian: Floral Patterns
Late Victorian: Art Nouveau Patterns

Early Victorian Patterns, 1835-1860

The earliest designs are predominantly Oriental motifs banking on the popularity of Chinese export porcelain. However, British and American historical views were also popular and scenic designs are found in the early flown pieces. These views were not realistic in their portrayal of places or events. They were romanticized versions of reality. Even country scenes were enhanced with sentimental devices designed to pluck Victorian heart strings.[7]

The Oriental views were also unrealistic. Decorative elements incorporating willow, bamboo, palm and apple trees, tea houses, pagodas, temples with upturned roofs, bridges, porches, towers, and tiny costumed figures, were all fused together to form a wide variety of pleasant but meaningless designs. Borders on the early plates were either stylized Far-Eastern or Arabic patterns. Some border patterns included small medallions repeating the center scene motif.[8]

Scenic designs, including this British Scenery soup bowl with a flanged rim, were found among the early Victorian period patterns. This piece dates from 1856, was manufactured by W. Davenport & Company, and measures 9 3/4" in diameter. *Courtesy of Louise and Charles Loehr, Louise's Old Things, Kutztown, Pennsylvania.* $55-75

The earliest designs were largely Oriental motifs such as this Chapoo platter dating from circa 1850. It was manufactured by John Wedge Wood and measures 13 5/8" x 10 1/2". *Courtesy of Louise and Charles Loehr, Louise's Old Things, Kutztown, Pennsylvania.* $300+

Late Victorian Patterns, 1880-the first quarter of the 20th century:

The Late Victorian patterns were predominantly Art Nouveau designs with a few medieval cathedrals thrown in for good measure. Art Nouveau styles were characterized by curved designs taken from the natural shapes of flowers and plants. Gone were the fancy finials, extravagant handles and excessive decorations of all kinds. This was stylized nature with a simplicity of design. Japanese art of this style was influential during this period as well.[10]

Through the last phase of Flow Blue production, floral transfer printed plates appeared by the thousands. Some were printed just on the rim, and some filled the plate. They were inexpensive to make and customers liked the varieties of buds, flowers, and sprays; this is the ware found predominantly at the end of the first quarter of the twentieth century.[11]

Throughout the periods there are also those pieces which defy classification because they combine several types, cutting and pasting design elements together in unique ways.

Middle Victorian period center motifs consisted predominantly of floral patterns. This example is a Nankin Jar pattern soup bowl dating from 1862, manufactured by G.L. Ashworth & Bros., and measuring 10 1/2" in diameter. *Courtesy of Louise and Charles Loehr, Louise's Old Things, Kutztown, Pennsylvania.* $75+

Middle Victorian Patterns, 1860-1880:

While occasional floral patterns appear on Early Victorian pieces, they are rare. During the Middle Victorian period, the predominant center motif is a floral pattern. However, artists also borrowed from many different sources and mixed and matched diverse elements as they pleased to create a variety of designs and held them all together with extravagant ornamentation. There are Oriental plates with European flowers or Gothic devices in the borders. Borders teeming with elaborate scroll work, shells and foliage or cartouches may be found. The cartouches are a series of medallions framing small scenes or bouquets. Occasionally added to all this are statues, columns, wreaths, and large imposing urns overflowing with trailing ferns and flowers. Variety and excessive decoration were the order of the day for the Middle Victorian period.[9]

Art Nouveau designs were common during the Late Victorian period. This example is an Aubrey pattern slop jar dating to 1903, manufactured by Doulton & Company, and measuring 11" tall and 11" in diameter. *Courtesy of Louise and Charles Loehr, Louise's Old Things, Kutztown, Pennsylvania.* $1500+ set

A few gothic cathedrals or their remains were thrown in including this Abbey pattern shredded wheat bowl dating to circa 1900, manufactured by George Jones & Sons Ltd., and measuring 6 1/4". *Courtesy of Louise and Charles Loehr, Louise's Old Things, Kutztown, Pennsylvania.* $70-120

Floral patterns also frequent the Late Victorian period including this Blenhiem pattern soup bowl dating from circa 1919, manufactured by Till & Sons, and measuring 9" in diameter. Courtesy of Linda Machalski, L.G. Antiques, Hartley, Delaware. $60-75

Dating Flow Blue with Manufacturers' Marks

Manufacturers' marks in Flow Blue usually provide the pattern name of the decoration and the manufacturer's name and / or symbol of the company. Marks were applied in many ways. These include scratching the unfired ware, impressing a stamp into the soft body, such as the Davenport anchor or Wedgwood name mark, painting the information on the surface before or after glazing, and, as described in Chapter 2, by using a transfer mark that is applied at the same time as the pattern and baked in the glaze kiln. The impressed stamp and transfer printed mark are the most common methods used on Flow Blue spieces.[12]

A great deal of information may by gleaned from manufacturers' marks by knowing when certain terms first appeared on specific marks. The following guidelines to marks will provide key elements of English and American marks. Look for them when dating Flow Blue ceramics up to and including the first quarter of the twentieth century.

1755: No impressed or printed name marks were in use prior to 1755.

1801: All printed marks occur after 1800.

1810: Any mark incorporating the name of the pattern post-dates 1810, and the majority occur much later.

1810: The English Royal Coat of Arms appear on marks after 1810.

1830: "published by" was used from roughly 1830 to 1840 and refers to the English 1797 Sculpture Copyright Act.

1838: Victorian quarter arms make their first appearance in 1838.

1840: Round or oval shaped garter-like marks are first used in 1840.

1842: Manufacturers' marks including diamond-shaped registration marks (discussed below) came into use in 1842 and ceased to be used after 1883. The registration mark was an English designation indicating that a design or process had been registered.

1850: The term "Royal" in the manufacturer's trade name was used on many English marks after 1850.

1855: Marks incorporating the word Limited or any standard abbreviations on English wares post-date and 1855 act establishing them and this coverage does not actually appear in use before the 1860s.

1859: The term "copyright" dates from 1859 to the present. It is usually a 20th century marks, however. It indicates a design, name or material is registered under United States copyright laws.

1863: From 1863 the term "Trade Mark" had been applied to English pieces in accord with the Trademark Act of 1862 and was applied to American wares after 1875.

1877: "copyright reserved" on a mark dates from 1877 and is a legal term used on English wares.

1880: The presence of "England" in the mark indicates a date after 1880, and generally after 1891, on exported wares.

1884: The presence of a registration number originates in 1884 (see below). It is the English designation which indicates that a design or process has been registered.

1887: "made in" begins use in 1887 and continues to be used.

English law required imported wares to be marked with these words and the country name.

1890s/1920s: "warranted" was used in several ways. There are three different uses of this term. In the United States and England it appears as part of the company name in the 1890s. It also is part of the term "warranted 22 karat gold," providing a guarantee to be real gold, in the 1920s.

1900: "Made in England" is a twentieth-century designation only required on wares exported from England. "Patented" occurs from 1900 onward. "Patented" signifies that a patent was granted by the United States Patent Office.

1901: After 1901 "U.S. patent" is used to denote that the design or method is patented in the United States. This term is also found on wares made outside the United States.

1902: "patent applied for" dates from 1902 to the present. It signifies that a patent application was filed with the United States Patent Office.

1900: semi-vitreous was used after 1901 and is another ironstone alias.

1903: The term "underglaze" dates from roughly 1903 to 1945 and signifies that the design is applied under the glaze.

1927: "designed expressly for" or "made expressly for" are terms originating in circa 1927 and continuing to the present day. Factorys sometimes made special patterns for use by one special customer. Those were frequently marked with the customer's name as well as the factory name.[13] Several examples are presented in Chapter 5.

When dating Flow Blue by the manufacturers' marks, there are a few points to be wary of. A date incorporated in a mark does not refer to the date of production. It usually signifies the year of the firm was established or generally to the establishment of a distant related predecessor. Additionally, many ceramic pieces from all periods were left unmarked and the absence of a mark does not necessarily indicate an early date. More often it simply means that the manufacturer's name was not well known and the inclusion of a mark would merely be a costly nuisance which would add nothing to the value of the ware. When presented with the absence of a mark, you need to rely on your knowledge of patterns, vessel forms and their periods of production instead.

Registration Marks

English registration marks are possibly the most complete and useful marks for dating any piece of English Flow Blue or other ceramic. Since 1842, English decorative art designs were registered at the British patent office, however, not every registered piece is marked.

A diamond-shaped mark was used between 1842 and 1883. The information within the diamond changed after 1867 and from 1884 on, the diamond-shaped marks were dropped in favor of registry numbers. Registry numbers (Rd. No.) indicating the year the piece was registered in a numeric sequence began in 1884 with the number 1. This date provides the earliest possible date of manufacture.[14]

In the 1842-1867 diamond-shaped mark, the letters and numbers indicate the following: the large Rd means "registered"; the Roman numeral in the circle at the top of the mark represents the type of material from which the piece is produced; the Roman numeral in the top inside section of the

diamond represents the year the piece was registered; the Arabic numeral on the right-hand section represents the day of the month the piece was registered; the Arabic numeral in the section at the bottom represents the parcel number, which is a code indicating the person or company who registered the piece, and the letter in the left-hand section represents the month the piece was registered.[15] For example:

In the 1868-1883 mark, the various numbers and their locations are changed to reflect the following: the large Rd and Roman Number remain unchanged; the Arabic numeral in

Registration mark indicating the year 1845 by the letter code "A" at the top of the diamond. *Courtesy of John and Nancy Harner, Dover Antique Mart, Smyrna, Delaware.*

the top inside section of the diamond represents the day of the month the piece was registered; the letter in the right-hand section represents the year the piece was registered; the letter in the bottom segment signifies the month the piece was registered; and the Arabic numeral at the left-hand side represents the parcel number.[16] The mark below was registered on September 4, 1879.

The registry mark is the second or late mark dating from 1868-1883. The Y code in the right hand point of the diamond indicates the year 1879, the D code at the base of the diamond indicates the month of September and the day of the month is located at the top of the diamond mark. This design was registered September 4, 1879. *Courtesy of Louise and Charles Loehr, Louise's Old Things, Kutztown, Pennsylvania.*

Chapter 5
Flow Blue Wares Through the Victorian Age

The Early Victorian Period: 1825-1860

AMOY Plate, 1844, by W. Davenport & Company, 7 1/4" in diameter. *Courtesy of Louise and Charles Loehr, Louise's Old Things, Kutztown, Pennsylvania.* $75+

ARABESQUE Sauce/Honey Dish, ca. 1845, by T. J. & J. Mayer, 5" diameter. *Courtesy of Louise and Charles Loehr, Louise's Old Things, Kutztown, Pennsylvania.* $100

W. Davenport & Company, Longport, Staffordshire, England, printed AMOY pattern name mark and anchor impress with the last two digits (44) of the year of manufacture on either side of the anchor, ca. 1800 - 1860. *Courtesy of Louise and Charles Loehr, Louise's Old Things, Kutztown, Pennsylvania.*

T. J. & J. Mayer, Longport, Staffordshire, England, printed animal mark with ARABESQUE pattern name, ca. 1843 to the mid-1850s. *Courtesy of Louise and Charles Loehr, Louise's Old Things, Kutztown, Pennsylvania.*

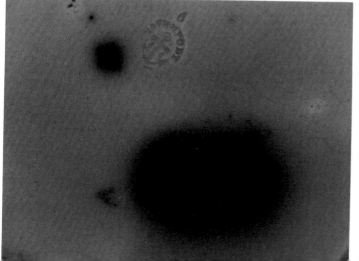

ATHENS Handleless Tea Cup with 12 side panels, 1840, by Charles Meigh but lacking any printed or impressed mark or pattern name. Handleless tea cups, or "tea bowls," were the first design manufactured by English potters, imitating the Chinese form as well as their pattern designs, 2 7/8" tall. *Courtesy of Louise and Charles Loehr, Louise's Old Things, Kutztown, Pennsylvania.* $85+

BEAUTIES OF CHINA Plate with a 14 panel rim, 1845, by Mellor, Venables & Company, 9 1/4" diameter. *Courtesy of Louise and Charles Loehr, Louise's Old Things, Kutztown, Pennsylvania.* $85+

Mellor, Venables & Company, Burslem, Staffordshire, England, printed initials mark with BEAUTIES OF CHINA pattern name, 1834 - 1851. *Courtesy of Louise and Charles Loehr, Louise's Old Things, Kutztown, Pennsylvania.*

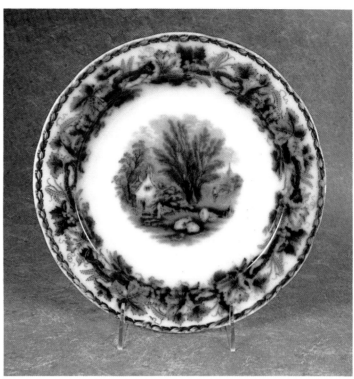

BRITISH SCENERY Soup Bowl with a flanged rim, 1856, by W. Davenport & Company, 9 3/4" diameter. *Courtesy of Louise and Charles Loehr, Louise's Old Things, Kutztown, Pennsylvania.* $55-75

W. Davenport & Company, Longport, Staffordshire, England, printed mark with BRITISH SCENERY pattern name, circa 1800 - 1860. *Courtesy of Louise and Charles Loehr, Louise's Old Things, Kutztown, Pennsylvania.*

W. Davenport & Company, Longport, Staffordshire, England, anchor impress included on the back of the BRITISH SCENERY soup bowl including the last two digits of the year (56) on eith side of the anchor, ca. 1800 - 1860. *Courtesy of Louise and Charles Loehr, Louise's Old Things, Kutztown, Pennsylvania.*

CANTON Platter, 1850, by John Maddock (Ltd.), 13 5/8" x 10 3/8". *Courtesy of Louise and Charles Loehr, Louise's Old Things, Kutztown, Pennsylvania.* $115-155

John Maddock (Ltd.), Burslem, Staffordshire, England, impressed mark used prior to 1855. After 1855 "& Son" was added to the mark. *Courtesy of Louise and Charles Loehr, Louise's Old Things, Kutztown, Pennsylvania.*

CANTON printed mark by John Maddock (Ltd.), found on reverse of the CANTON platter dating prior to 1855. *Courtesy of Louise and Charles Loehr, Louise's Old Things, Kutztown, Pennsylvania.*

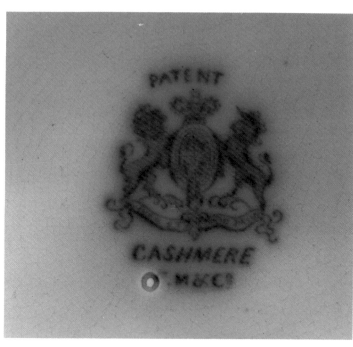

CASHMERE Plate with 10 panels, circa 1850, Francis Morley & Company, 9 1/4" in diameter. *Courtesy of Jacqueline Hunsicker.* $150+

Francis Morley & Company, Hanley, Staffordshire, England, printed British Royal Arms mark, manufacturer's initials and CASHMERE pattern name, circa 1845 - 1858. *Courtesy of Jacqueline Hunsicker.*

CASHMERE Wash Pitcher and Basin, circa 1842 - 1844, by Ridgway & Morley. Toilet sets included a wash pitcher (ewer) and basin, soap dish, sponge dish, a cup for brushing teeth, and a chamber pot. Sets were produced by many firms and were at the height of their manufacture from 1860 - 1910. As you continue you will find examples of each piece in of a toilet set. This is also a good example of successive manufacturers using the same pattern design and name. Pitcher 11 1/8" tall and wash basin 13 3/4" in diameter. *Courtesy of Bonne Hohl.* $2500+

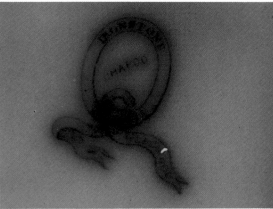

CASHMERE Soap Dish and Drainer, circa 1842 - 1844, by Ridgway & Morley. Note that the pattern is continued inside the soap dish on the drainer. 7 3/4" x 5 1/2" x 2". *Courtesy of Bonne Hohl.* $1200+

John Wedge Wood, Burslem & Tunstall, Staffordshire, England, printed oval banner mark with pattern name, 1841 - 1860. Notice that this is not the mark of Josiah Wedgwood; Josiah never included his first initial in his marks. Of course, any confusion over the spelling of the name on the mark was sure not to do John Wedge Wood's business any harm. *Courtesy of Louise and Charles Loehr, Louise's Old Things, Kutztown, Pennsylvania.*

Ridgway & Morley, Hanley, Staffordshire, England, printed British Royal Arms mark with R & M initials and CASHMERE pattern name, circa 1842 - 1844. *Courtesy of Bonne Hohl.*

CHAPOO Plate with 12 panel rim, circa 1850, by John Wedge Wood, 7 1/2" in diameter. *Courtesy of Jacqueline Hunsicker.* $80-100

CHAPOO Platter, circa 1850, by John Wedge Wood, 13 5/8" x 10 1/2". *Courtesy of Louise and Charles Loehr, Louise's Old Things, Kutztown, Pennsylvania.* $300+

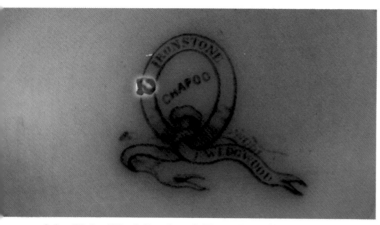

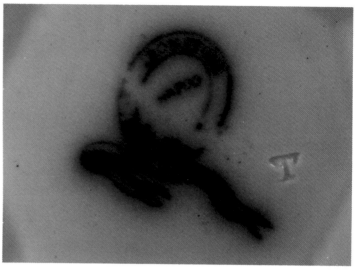

John Wedge Wood, Burslem & Tunstall, Staffordshire, England, printed oval banner mark with pattern name, 1841 - 1860. *Courtesy of Jacqueline Hunsicker.*

CHAPOO Teapot, 2 quart capacity with 8 body panels, 1850, by John Wedge Wood, 9 1/4" tall. *Courtesy of Louise and Charles Loehr, Louise's Old Things, Kutztown, Pennsylvania.* $650+

John Wedge Wood, Burslem & Tunstall, Staffordshire, England, printed oval banner mark with pattern name, 1841 - 1860. *Courtesy of Louise and Charles Loehr, Louise's Old Things, Kutztown, Pennsylvania.*

CHEN-SI Platter, circa 1812-1836, by John Meir, 13 1/2" x 10 3/8". *Courtesy of Louise and Charles Loehr, Louise's Old Things, Kutztown, Pennsylvania.* $250+

CHEN-SI Handleless Coffee Cup and Saucer with 12 side panels, 1835, by John Meir. The cup measures 3 1/4" tall and 3 5/8" in diameter. The saucer measures 6 1/4" in diameter. *Courtesy of Louise and Charles Loehr, Louise's Old Things, Kutztown, Pennsylvania.* $150+

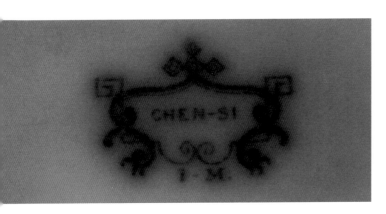

John Meir, Tunstall, Staffordshire, England, printed initials appear as I. M. but are indeed an early John Meir mark, 1812 - 1836. *Courtesy of Louise and Charles Loehr, Louise's Old Things, Kutztown, Pennsylvania.*

John Meir, Tunstall, Staffordshire, England. Printed initials appear as I. M. but are indeed an early John Meir mark, 1812 - 1836. *Courtesy of Louise and Charles Loehr, Louise's Old Things, Kutztown, Pennsylvania.*

John Goodwin, Longton, Staffordshire, England, printed initials in banner mark with CHIANG pattern name, 1841-1851. *Courtesy of Arnold A. Kowalsky.*

CHIANG polychrome teapot, c. 1841, John Goodwin. 8" high to finial. *Courtesy of Arnold A. Kowalsky.* $700+.

CIRCASSIA Handleless Cup, 1840, J. & G. Alcock with no printed or impressed mark, 3 3/4" tall and 2 3/4" in diameter. *Courtesy of Louise and Charles Loehr, Louise's Old Things, Kutztown, Pennsylvania.* $85+

COLUMBIA Cup Plate with 12 paneled rim, 1846, Clementson & Young with no printed or impressed mark, 4" in diameter. *Courtesy of Louise and Charles Loehr, Louise's Old Things, Kutztown, Pennsylvania.* $100+

GOTHIC Charger, 1844, by W. Davenport & Company, 13 7/8" in diameter. *Courtesy of Louise and Charles Loehr, Louise's Old Things, Kutztown, Pennsylvania.* $250+

EXCELSIOR Teapot with 12 side panels, circa 1850, no printed or impressed mark but possibly T. F. & Company, 8 1/2" tall. *Courtesy of Jacqueline Hunsicker.* $650+

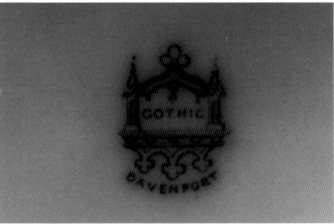

W. Davenport & Company, Longport, Staffordshire, England, printed mark with GOTHIC pattern name and impressed Davenport anchor with the last digits (44) of the year of manufacture, circa 1793 - 1887. *Courtesy of Louise and Charles Loehr, Louise's Old Things, Kutztown, Pennsylvania.*

CHINESE footbath by Thomas Dimmock & Company, Shelton, Staffordshire, c. 1828-1859. *Courtesy of Suzanne and William Hagenlocher, Castleton, Vermont.* $3500-4500.

HONG KONG Covered Vegetable Dish, circa 1845, by Charles Meigh, a rare and elegant piece, 6" tall x 8 1/8" in diameter. *Courtesy of Bonne Hohl.* $600+

HONG KONG Covered (possible) Hot Milk Pitcher, circa 1845, by Charles Meigh, a profile view of a rare piece in this pattern, 7 1/2" tall. *Courtesy of Bonne Hohl.* $800+

HONG KONG Covered (possible) Hot Milk Pitcher, circa 1845, by Charles Meigh, another rare piece in this pattern, 7 1/2" tall. *Courtesy of Bonne Hohl.* $900-1200

HONG KONG Ewer and Wash Basin, circa 1845, by Charles Meigh. The ewer measures 11" tall and the wash basin measures 7 7/8" in diameter. *Courtesy of Bonne Hohl.* $1500+

HONG KONG Tooth Brush Holders, circa 1845, by Charles Meigh. Note the continuation of the pattern on the interior of the piece. These holders measure 7 7/8" x 3 1/4". *Courtesy of Bonne Hohl.* $600+ ea.

F. & R. Pratt, Fenton, Staffordshire, England, printed INDIAN pattern name, circa 1818 - present. *Courtesy of Louise and Charles Loehr, Louise's Old Things, Kutztown, Pennsylvania.*

HONG KONG Shaving Mug, circa 1845, by Charles Meigh, 2 7/8" tall and 2 3/4" in diameter. *Courtesy of Bonne Hohl.* $350+

INDIAN Handleless Tea Cup and Saucer, circa 1840, by F. & R. Pratt. The cup measures 3" tall and 3 3/4" in diameter. The saucer measures 5 7/8" in diameter. *Courtesy of Louise and Charles Loehr, Louise's Old Things, Kutztown, Pennsylvania.* $150+

INDIAN Sugar Bowl with Lid, circa 1840, by F. & R. Pratt . This is an unusual faceted design. The open handles repeat the faceted design. Sugar bowls like this one were very large until the middle 1860s because sugar was molded and sold in a conical loaves. The loaves were cut into pieces and placed in these large, wide mouthed bowls. With the introduction of granulated sugar, the sugar bowls rapidly shrank to the shapes we are familiar with today. This sugar bowl measures 8" tall and 5" in diameter at the mouth. *Courtesy of Louise and Charles Loehr, Louise's Old Things, Kutztown, Pennsylvania.* $400+

INDIAN JAR Plate with 12 paneled rim, circa 1843, by Jacob &
Thomas Furnival, 10 1/4" in diameter. *Courtesy of Jacqueline
Hunsicker.* $110+

INDIAN JAR Platter, circa 1844 - 1846, by Thomas Furnival
and Company, 12 3/4" x 9 1/4". *Courtesy of Jacqueline Hunsicker.*
$300+

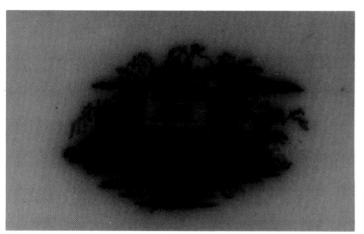

Thomas Furnival & Company, Hanley, Staffordshire, England,
printed scroll mark with T. F. & C. manufacturer's initials and
INDIAN JAR pattern name, circa 1844 - 1846. *Courtesy of
Jacqueline Hunsicker.*

Jacob & Thomas Furnival, Hanley, Staffordshire, England, printed
scroll, manufacturer's initials and INDIAN JAR pattern name,
circa 1843 - 1964. *Courtesy of Jacqueline Hunsicker.*

INDIAN JAR Soup Bowl, circa 1843, by Jacob & Thomas Furnival.
The shape of this particular soup bowl is peculiar for this period, it
has a round rather than a paneled rim. The bowl measures 9 1/2" in
diameter. *Courtesy of Jacqueline Hunsicker.* $125+

Jacob & Thomas Furnival, Hanley, Staffordshire, England, printed scroll, manufacturer's initials and INDIAN JAR pattern name, circa 1843 - 1964. *Courtesy of Jacqueline Hunsicker.*

Thomas Furnival & Company, Hanley, Staffordshire, England, printed scroll mark with T. F. & C. manufacturer's initials and INDIAN JAR pattern name, circa 1844 - 1846. *Courtesy of Jacqueline Hunsicker.*

INDIAN JAR Vegetable Dish without a lid, circa 1843 - 1846, no mark or pattern name, 11" x 10" x 3 1/2". *Courtesy of Jacqueline Hunsicker.* $200

INDIAN JAR Soup Tureen with Underplate, circa 1844 - 1846, by Thomas Furnival and Company. The missing ladle is a common occurrence. The tureen measures 11 3/4" x 8 1/2" x 11". The underplate measures 13" x 11". *Courtesy of Jacqueline Hunsicker.* $2200+

INDIAN JAR Sauce Tureen without Ladle, circa 1843 - 1846, no mark or pattern name, 6" x 4" x 6". *Courtesy of Jacqueline Hunsicker.* $625+

INDIAN JAR Gravy Boat, circa 1843 - 1846, no mark or pattern name, 7" x 3" x 3". *Courtesy of Jacqueline Hunsicker.* $275-325

INDIAN JAR Pitcher with 6 paneled sides, circa 1843 - 1846, no mark or pattern name. This is a serving pitcher and measures 7" tall. *Courtesy of Jacqueline Hunsicker.* $600+

INDIAN JAR Creamer, circa 1843 - 1846, no mark or pattern name, 5 1/2" tall. *Courtesy of Jacqueline Hunsicker.* $400-500

INDIAN JAR Sugar Bowl and Teapot, circa 1843 - 1846, no mark or pattern name. Shown together it is easy to see just how large sugar bowls were prior to 1860. The sugar bowl measures 7 1/2" tall with a 5 1/2" diameter mouth. The teapot measures 8 3/4" tall. *Courtesy of Jacqueline Hunsicker.* $1100+ set

INDIAN JAR Tea Cup and Saucer, circa 1844 - 1846, by Thomas Furnival and Company. The tea cup measures 2 1/2" tall and 3 7/8" in diameter. The saucer measures 6" in diameter. *Courtesy of Jacqueline Hunsicker.* $200+

INDIAN JAR Waste Bowl, circa 1844 - 1846, by Thomas Furnival and Company. The waste bowl measures 4" tall and 6 1/2" in diameter. *Courtesy of Jacqueline Hunsicker.* $300

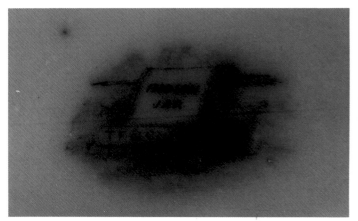

Thomas Furnival & Company, Hanley, Staffordshire, England, printed scroll mark with T. F. & C. manufacturer's initials and INDIAN JAR pattern name, circa 1844 - 1846. *Courtesy of Jacqueline Hunsicker.*

LAHORE Teapot, circa 1840, no mark or pattern name but possibly manufactured by T. Phillips and Son of Burslem, Staffordshire, England, 10" tall. *Courtesy of Jacqueline Hunsicker.* $700+

INDIAN JAR Sylibub (Punch) Cup, circa 1843 - 1846, no mark or pattern name, 3" tall and 3" in diameter. *Courtesy of Jacqueline Hunsicker.* $225+

LINTIN Cup Plate, 1845, no mark or pattern name but attributed to Thomas Godwin of Burslem, Staffordshire, England, 4" in diameter. *Courtesy of Louise and Charles Loehr, Louise's Old Things, Kutztown, Pennsylvania.* $100+

LOBELIA Platter, 1845, by George Phillips, 13 1/2" x 10 1/2". *Courtesy of John and Nancy Harner, Dover Antique Mart, Smyrna, Delaware.* $200+

George Phillips, Longport, Staffordshire, England, printed banner and registration mark indicating the year 1845 by the letter code "A" at the top of the diamond. The registration mark was a device used from 1842 to 1883 to indicated that the design or shape had been registered with the Patent Office in London, providing the collector with the earliest possible year of manufacture. After 1883 a registration number (Rd. No.) code replaced the registration mark. The G. Phillips banner mark was used from circa 1834 - 1848. *Courtesy of John and Nancy Harner, Dover Antique Mart, Smyrna, Delaware.*

MANDARIN Drainer, 1840, by F. & R. Pratt & Company, 12" x 9". *Courtesy of Louise and Charles Loehr, Louise's Old Things, Kutztown, Pennsylvania.* $300+

MANILLA Plate, 1845, by Podmore, Walker & Company, 8 5/8" in diameter. *Courtesy of Louise and Charles Loehr, Louise's Old Things, Kutztown, Pennsylvania.* $75-95

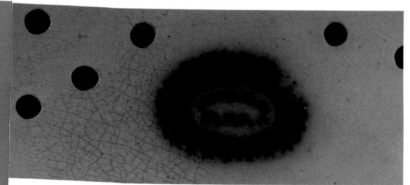

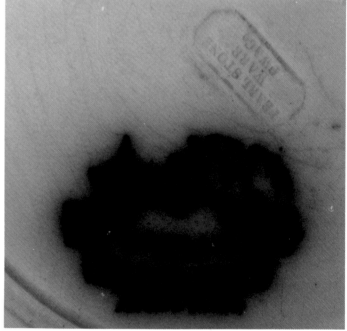

F. & R. Pratt Company, Fenton, Staffordshire, England, printed manufacturer's name and MANDARIN pattern name, circa 1818 - 1860. *Courtesy of Louise and Charles Loehr, Louise's Old Things, Kutztown, Pennsylvania.*

Podmore, Walker & Company, Tunstall, Staffordshire, England, printed and impressed manufacturer's initials and MANILLA pattern name. It is interesting to note that the plate is described as ironstone in the printed mark and by one of its many aliases, "pearl stone ware" (not to be confused with the earlier pearlware), in the impressed mark. The manufacturer's initials P. W. & Co. were used as identification from 1834 - 1859. *Courtesy of Louise and Charles Loehr, Louise's Old Things, Kutztown, Pennsylvania.*

TONQUIN Bowl, circa 1845 - 1853, William Adams & Sons, 8 3/8" in diameter. *Courtesy of Marion Butz, The Antique Marketplace, Lancaster, Pennsylvania.* $85-110

Unidentified Butter Pat, circa 1835 - 1847, by Charles Meigh, 4" in diameter. *Courtesy of Louise and Charles Loehr, Louise's Old Things, Kutztown, Pennsylvania.* $50+

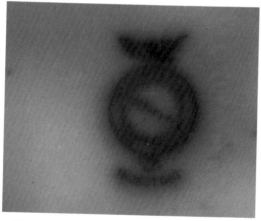

William Adams & Sons Ltd., Tunstall & Stoke, Staffordshire, England, circular printed mark with manufacturer's name along the upper border and TONQUIN pattern name in center of mark, 1769 - present. *Courtesy of Marion Butz, The Antique Marketplace, Lancaster, Pennsylvania.*

Charles Meigh, Hanley, Staffordshire, England, impressed mark with IMPROVED STONE CHINA in the center of the mark, 1835 -1849. This mark was also used by J. Meigh & Sons and Charles Meigh & Son. *Courtesy of Louise and Charles Loehr, Louise's Old Things, Kutztown, Pennsylvania.*

TROY Relish Dish, circa 1840, by Charles Meigh, no printed or incised mark or pattern name, 8 3/4" x 5". *Courtesy of Linda Machalski, L. G. Antiques, Hartley, Delaware.* $150+

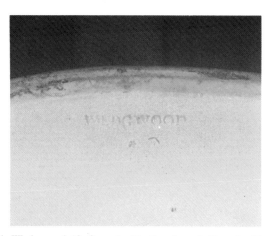

Unidentified Chinese Patterned Footbath, circa 1850, by Josiah Wedgwood, 15 7/8" x 12 3/4" x 8 1/2". Footbaths are difficult to find and draw a high price, especially in excellent condition as illustrated here. *Courtesy of Bonne Hohl.* $1500+

Josiah Wedgwood (& Sons Ltd.), Burslem & Etrutia, England, impressed manufacturer's name, from circa 1759 - 1859. *Courtesy of Bonne Hohl.*

Unidentified Floral Patterned Plate, circa 1840, F. & R. Pratt & Company, 10 1/4" in diameter. *Courtesy of Louise and Charles Loehr, Louise's Old Things, Kutztown, Pennsylvania.* $125

F. & R. Pratt & Company, Fenton, Staffordshire, England, the printed company initials date the mark to circa 1840 - 1860. The No. 9 mark indicates the company's pattern number in lieu of a name. *Courtesy of Louise and Charles Loehr, Louise's Old Things, Kutztown, Pennsylvania.*

Podmore Walker & Company, Tunstall, Staffordshire, England, printed and impressed mark with company initials and printed WASHINGTON VASE pattern name, 1849 - 1859. *Courtesy of Linda Machalski, L. G. Antiques, Hartley, Delaware.*

WASHINGTON VASE Plate, circa 1849 - 1859, Podmore Walker & Company, 10" in diameter. *Courtesy of Linda Machalski, L. G. Antiques, Hartley, Delaware.* $125

The Middle Victorian Period: 1860-1880

CEYLON Pedestal Compote, 1876, by Furnival, 11" x 7 1/2" x 5 4/5". *Courtesy of Louise and Charles Loehr, Louise's Old Things, Kutztown, Pennsylvania.* $150-200

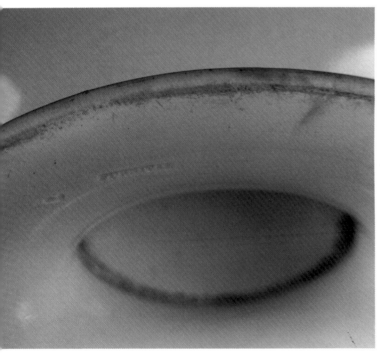

Thomas Furnival & Sons, Cobridge, Staffordshire, England, impressed manufacturer's name, 1871 - 1890. *Courtesy of Louise and Charles Loehr, Louise's Old Things, Kutztown, Pennsylvania.*

COBURG Plate with 12 panel rim, 1860, by John Edwards, 10 1/2" in diameter. *Courtesy of Louise and Charles Loehr, Louise's Old Things, Kutztown, Pennsylvania.* $150

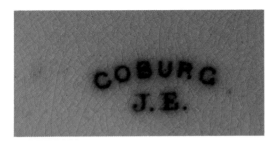

James Edwards, Fenton, Staffordshire, England, with printed manufacturer's initials mark and pattern name, 1847 - 1873, "& Co." was added to the mark from circa 1873 - 1879. *Courtesy of Louise and Charles Loehr, Louise's Old Things, Kutztown, Pennsylvania.*

James Edwards, Fenton, Staffordshire, England, no printed or impressed manufacturer's initials mark, printed FLENSBURG pattern name, circa 1847 - 1879. *Courtesy of Bonne Hohl.*

COBURG Teapot with 8 panel sides, circa 1860, no printed or incised mark or pattern name, 6 1/2" tall. *Courtesy of Jacqueline Hunsicker.* $600+

FLENSBURG Plate with 12 panel rim, circa 1865, by James Edwards, 10" in diameter. A very different look in Flow Blue with polychrome underglaze designs—an eagle, urn, and floral center motif. There is also very little visible flowing of the colors. *Courtesy of Bonne Hohl.* $65-85

FLENSBURG Plate with 12 panel rim, circa 1865, by James Edwards, 9" in diameter. Courtesy of Bonne Hohl. $60-80

Opposite page top:
FLENSBURG Vegetable Dish, circa 1865, by James Edwards, 9 3/4" x 7". *Courtesy of Bonne Hohl.* $80-100

Opposite page bottom:
FLENSBURG Platter, circa 1865, by James Edwards, 13 3/4" x 10 1/2". *Courtesy of Bonne Hohl.* $125-175

FLENSBURG Covered Vegetable Dish, circa 1865, by James
Edwards, 11" x 8 1/4" x 7". *Courtesy of Bonne Hohl.* $225-275

FLENSBURG Tea Cups, Saucers and Cup Plate, circa 1865, by James Edwards. Left to right: Tea Cup with
Handle and 8 side panels, 2 3/4" tall x 3 3/4" in diameter; Saucers, 6" in diameter; Handleless Tea Cup with
8 side panels, 2 3/4" tall x 3 3/4" in diameter; Handleless Tea Cup with round sides, 3" tall x 3 1/2" in
diameter; and Cup Plate, 3 3/4" in diameter. *Courtesy of Bonne Hohl.* $85-105 per set

FLENSBURG Teapot, circa 1865, by James Edwards, 9" tall. *Courtesy of Bonne Hohl.* $250-325

FRANCE Soup Plate with Broad Rounded Rim, 1879, by Brown, Westhead, Moore & Company, 10 1/4" in diameter. *Courtesy of Louise and Charles Loehr, Louise's Old Things, Kutztown, Pennsylvania.* $35-55

FLENSBURG Pitcher, circa 1865, by James Edwards. This is a serving pitcher measuring 7" tall. *Courtesy of Bonne Hohl.* $200-250

Brown, Westhead, Moore & Company, Hanley, Staffordshire, England, printed crown and shield mark including manufacturer's initials and FRANCE pattern name. The registry mark is the second or late mark dating from 1868 - 1883. The Y code in the right hand point of the diamond indicates the year 1879, the D code at the base of the diamond indicates the month of September and the day of the month is located at the top of the diamond mark. This design was registered September 4, 1879. *Courtesy of Louise and Charles Loehr, Louise's Old Things, Kutztown, Pennsylvania.*

JENNY LIND Bowl, 1860, by Charles Meigh & Son, 2 1/2" tall x 5" in diameter. *Courtesy of Louise and Charles Loehr, Louise's Old Things, Kutztown, Pennsylvania.* $150+

KIRKEE Plate with 14 panel rim, circa 1861, by John Meir & Son, 10" in diameter. Courtesy of Linda Machalski, L. G. Antiques, Hartley, Delaware. $110+

JENNY LIND Bowl with Wood Base and Silver Crest, Rim and Bail, 1860, by Charles Meigh & Son. *Courtesy of Louise and Charles Loehr, Louise's Old Things, Kutztown, Pennsylvania.* $250+

KIRKEE Handleless Cup and Saucer, circa 1861, by John Meir & Son. The cup measures 3" tall x 3 3/4" in diameter and the saucer measures 6" in diameter. *Courtesy of Jacqueline Hunsicker.* $150

John Meir & Son, Tunstall, Staffordshire, England, printed circle and crown mark with J. Meir & Son name at top of circle and KIRKEE pattern name in circle's center, 1837 - 1897. *Courtesy of Jacqueline Hunsicker.*

Charles Meigh & Son, Hanley, Staffordshire, England, printed mark with manufacturer's initials (C.M.&S.) and JENNY LIND pattern name, 1851 - 1861. *Courtesy of Louise and Charles Loehr, Louise's Old Things, Kutztown, Pennsylvania.*

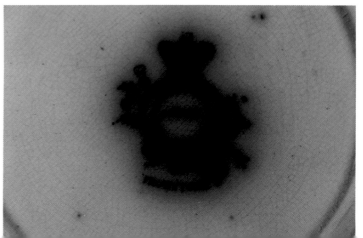

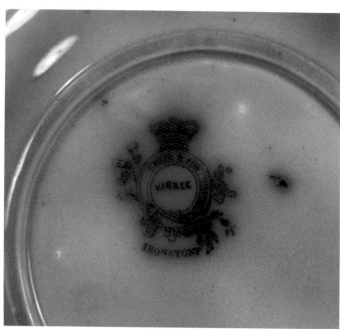

KIRKEE Tea Cup and Saucer, circa 1861, John Meir & Son. The cup measures 3" tall x 3 5/8" in diameter. The saucer measures 6 1/4" in diameter. This piece is heavily flown. *Courtesy of Linda Machalski, L. G. Antiques, Hartley, Delaware.* $200+

John Meir & Son, Tunstall, Staffordshire, England, printed circle and crown mark with J. Meir & Son name at top of circle and KIRKEE pattern name in circle's center, 1837 - 1897. *Courtesy of Linda Machalski, L. G. Antiques, Hartley, Delaware.*

KIRKEE (left to right) Sugar Bowl, Teapot and Cream Pitcher with 8 panel sides, circa 1861, by John Meir & Son. The sugar bowl measures 8" tall, the teapot measures 9" tall, and the cream pitcher measures 5" tall. *Courtesy of Jacqueline Hunsicker.* $1600+

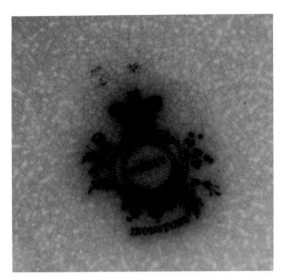

John Meir & Son, Tunstall, Staffordshire, England, printed circle and crown mark with J. Meir & Son name at top of circle and KIRKEE pattern name in circle's center, 1837 - 1897. *Courtesy of Jacqueline Hunsicker.*

KIRKEE Pedestaled Center Piece, circa 1861, by John Meir & Son, 6" tall x 9 3/4" in diameter. The center design is found complete in the center of the bowl. *Courtesy of Jacqueline Hunsicker.* $1100+

KIRKEE Pedestaled Center Piece, circa 1861, by John Meir & Son, 6" tall x 9 3/4" in diameter. *Courtesy of Jacqueline Hunsicker.* $1100+

John Meir & Son, Tunstall, Staffordshire, England, printed circle and crown mark with J. Meir & Son name at top of circle and KIRKEE pattern name in circle's center, 1837 - 1897. *Courtesy of Jacqueline Hunsicker.*

KYBER Platter, circa 1870, by John Meir & Sons with no printed or impressed mark or pattern name, 18" x 14". *Courtesy of Louise and Charles Loehr, Louise's Old Things, Kutztown, Pennsylvania.* $500-700

KYBER 2 Qt. Pitcher with 8 side panels, circa 1870, by John Meir & Sons, 9 1/2" tall. Courtesy of Jacqueline Hunsicker. $700+

John Meir & Son, Tunstall, Staffordshire, England, printed circle and crown mark with J. Meir & Son name at top of circle and KYBER pattern name in circle's center, 1837 - 1897. *Courtesy of Jacqueline Hunsicker.*

LATE SPODE Plate, 1867, by Copeland, 10" in diameter. *Courtesy of Louise and Charles Loehr, Louise's Old Things, Kutztown, Pennsylvania.* $80-100

LUSTRE BAND Plate, 1860, by Elsmore & Forster, 10" in diameter. *Courtesy of Louise and Charles Loehr, Louise's Old Things, Kutztown, Pennsylvania.* $40-60

W. T. Copeland (& Sons Ltd.), Stoke, Staffordshire, England, printed manufacturer's name and LATE SPODE pattern name, circa 1847 - 1867. *Courtesy of Louise and Charles Loehr, Louise's Old Things, Kutztown, Pennsylvania.*

Elsmore & Forster, Tunstall, Staffordshire, England, impressed mark with manufacturer's name, 1853 - 1871. *Courtesy of Louise and Charles Loehr, Louise's Old Things, Kutztown, Pennsylvania.*

LUSTRE BAND Plate, 1860, by Elsmore & Forster, 8 3/4" in diameter. *Courtesy of Linda Machalski, L. G. Antiques, Hartley, Delaware.* $35-55

Elsmore & Forster, Tunstall, Staffordshire, England, impressed mark with manufacturer's initials (E-F & Co.), 1853 - 1871. *Courtesy of Linda Machalski, L. G. Antiques, Hartley, Delaware.*

SHANGHAE Plate, 1870, by Jacob Furnival & Company, 9" in diameter. *Courtesy of Louise and Charles Loehr, Louise's Old Things, Kutztown, Pennsylvania.* $100+

NANKIN JAR Soup Bowl with large rim, 1862, by G. L. Ashworth & Bros., 10 1/2" in diameter. *Courtesy of Louise and Charles Loehr, Louise's Old Things, Kutztown, Pennsylvania.* $100

G. L. Ashworth & Bros., Hanley, Staffordshire, England, impressed manufacturer's name (ASHWORTH) and printed NANKIN JAR pattern name, 1862 - 1880. *Courtesy of Louise and Charles Loehr, Louise's Old Things, Kutztown, Pennsylvania.*

SHANGHAE Plate, 1870, by Jacob Furnival & Company, 8 3/8" in diameter. *Courtesy of Louise and Charles Loehr, Louise's Old Things, Kutztown, Pennsylvania.* $75-95

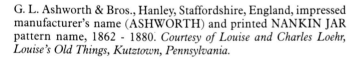

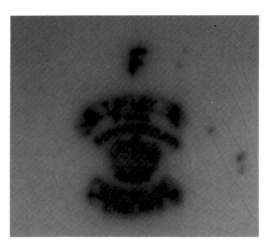

Wood & Son(s Ltd.), Burslem, Staffordshire, England, printed crown and banner mark with manufacturer's name within the banner below the crown and the TRILBY pattern name within the upper banner, 1891 - 1907. *Courtesy of Jacqueline Hunsicker.*

ARCADIA Saucer, circa 1907, by Arthur J. Wilkinson, Burslem, Staffordshire, England, 4 3/4" in diameter. *Courtesy of Linda Machalski, L. G. Antiques, Hartley, Delaware.* $25+

ALBANY Soap Dish with Drain Insert, circa 1891 - 1914, by W. H. Grindley & Company, 3 1/2" tall x 4 3/4" in diameter. *Courtesy of Jacqueline Hunsicker.* $150-250

Arthur J. Wilkinson, Royal Staffordshire Pottery, Burslem, Staffordshire, England, printed mark with company name within banner and ARCADIA pattern name, circa 1907. *Courtesy of Linda Machalski, L. G. Antiques, Hartley, Delaware.*

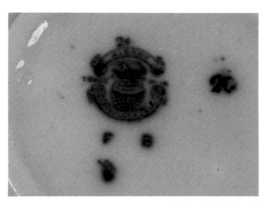

W. H. Grindley & Company Ltd., Tunstall, Staffordshire, England, printed globe and ship mark surrounded by banners with manufacturer's name in the lower banner and ALBANY pattern name in the upper banner, circa 1891 - 1914. *Courtesy of Jacqueline Hunsicker.*

ARCADIA Tureen without Ladle, circa 1907, Arthur J. Wilkinson, 6" tall x 10 1/2" in diameter. *Courtesy of John and Nancy Harner, Dover Antique Mart, Smyrna, Delaware.* $350

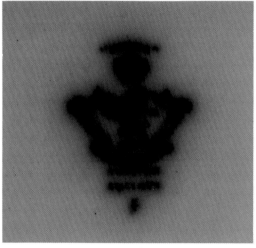

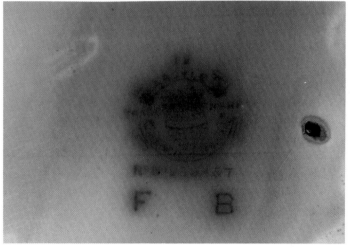

Arthur J. Wilkinson, Royal Staffordshire Pottery, Burslem, Staffordshire, England, printed mark with company name within banner and ARCADIA pattern name, circa 1907. *Courtesy of John and Nancy Harner, Dover Antique Mart, Smyrna, Delaware.*

ARGYLE Platter, circa 1891 - 1914, W. H. Grindley & Company, 15 1/4" x 11". *Courtesy of Linda Machalski, L. G. Antiques, Hartley, Delaware.* $250+

W. H. Grindley & Company Ltd., Tunstall, Staffordshire, England, printed globe and ship mark surrounded by banners with manufacturer's name in the lower banner and ARGYLE pattern name in the upper banner, circa 1891 - 1914. *Courtesy of Linda Machalski, L. G. Antiques, Hartley, Delaware.*

ARVISTA Salad Bowl with Salad Fork and Spoon, circa 1894, by W. R. Carlton. Set had silver trim and utensils. The salad bowl measures 4" tall x 7 1/2" in diameter. The utensils measure 10 3/4" in length. *Courtesy of Jacqueline Hunsicker.* $250+

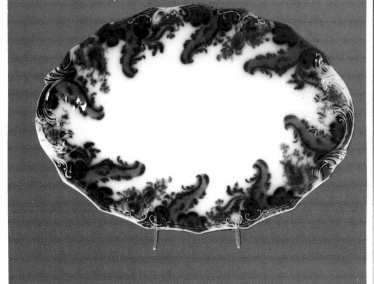

Wilton & Robinson/Carlton Ware Ltd., Stoke, Staffordshire, England, printed crown and circle mark with manufacturer's name and ARVISTA pattern name, circa 1894. *Courtesy of Jacqueline Hunsicker.*

ATALANTA Platter, circa 1906, by Wedgwood & Company, 14" x 10 1/2". *Courtesy of Jacqueline Hunsicker.* $125+

ASIATIC PHEASANTS Relish Tray, circa 1895, Thomas Hughes & Sons (Ltd.), 8 3/8" x 4 1/2". *Courtesy of Louise and Charles Loehr, Louise's Old Things, Kutztown, Pennsylvania.* $125+

Wedgwood & Company Ltd., Tunstall, Staffordshire, England, printed crown mark with manufacturer's name and ATALANTA pattern name, circa 1906. *Courtesy of Jacqueline Hunsicker.*

Thomas Hughes & Sons (Ltd.), Burslem, Staffordshire, England, printed mark with manufacturer's initials (TH & SONS) and ASIATIC PHEASANT pattern name, circa 1895 - 1910. *Courtesy of Louise and Charles Loehr, Louise's Old Things, Kutztown, Pennsylvania.*

ATHOL Cup and Saucer, circa 1898, possibly by Burgess & Leigh although no mark is present. The cup measures 2 1/2" tall x 3 1/2" in diameter and the saucer measures 6" in diameter. *Courtesy of John and Nancy Harner, Dover Antique Mart, Smyrna, Delaware.* $50+

ATHOL pattern name without a mark. The registration number (Rd No.) supplies the pattern registration date as 1898. *Courtesy of John and Nancy Harner, Dover Antique Mart, Smyrna, Delaware.*

AUBREY Sponge and Soap Dish, 1903, by Doulton & Company, 3" tall x 7 3/8" in diameter. The removable soap dish rests on top of the sponge in the two-handled bowl beneath. *Courtesy of Louise and Charles Loehr, Louise's Old Things, Kutztown, Pennsylvania.* $1500+ set

AUBREY Wash Pitcher and Basin, 1903, by Doulton & Company. The pitcher measures 13 1/4" tall and the basin measures 16" in diameter. *Courtesy of Louise and Charles Loehr, Louise's Old Things, Kutztown, Pennsylvania.* $1500+ set

AUBREY Chamber Pot, 1903, by Doulton & Company, 5 1/2" tall x 9 1/4" in diameter. *Courtesy of Louise and Charles Loehr, Louise's Old Things, Kutztown, Pennsylvania.* $1500+ set

Doulton & Company, Burslem, Staffordshire & Lambeth, London, England, printed mark was used from 1902 - 1930. The registration number code indicates the year of registration was 1903. Printed AUBREY pattern name. *Courtesy of Louise and Charles Loehr, Louise's Old Things, Kutztown, Pennsylvania.*

AUBREY Slop Jar with Reed Handle and Insert, 1903, by Doulton & Company, 11" tall x 11" in diameter. *Courtesy of Louise and Charles Loehr, Louise's Old Things, Kutztown, Pennsylvania.* $1500+ set

AYR Saucer, circa 1900 - 1904, by W. & E. Corn, 6" in diameter. *Courtesy of Linda Machalski, L. G. Antiques, Hartley, Delaware.* $30+

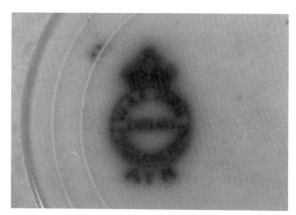

W. & E. Corn, Longport, Staffordshire, England, printed crown and circle mark with manufacturer's name and AYR pattern name, circa 1900 - 1904. *Courtesy of Linda Machalski, L. G. Antiques, Hartley, Delaware.*

AYR Cup and Saucer, circa 1900 - 1904, by W. & E. Corn. The cup measures 2 1/2" tall x 3 3/8" in diameter. The saucer measures 6" in diameter. *Courtesy of Linda Machalski, L. G. Antiques, Hartley, Delaware.* $65+

W. & E. Corn, Longport, Staffordshire, England, printed crown and circle mark with manufacturer's name and AYR pattern name, circa 1900 - 1904. *Courtesy of Linda Machalski, L. G. Antiques, Hartley, Delaware.*

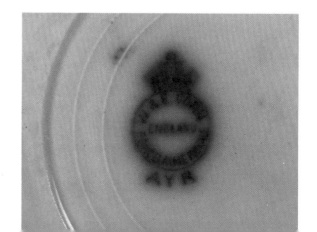

BALMORAL Plate, 1890, by J. & G. Meakin, 10" in diameter. *Courtesy of Linda Machalski, L. G. Antiques, Hartley, Delaware.* $50+

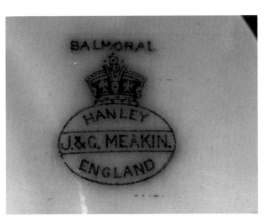

J. & G. Meakin (Ltd.), Hanley, Staffordshire, England, printed crown and oval mark with manufacturer's name and BALMORAL pattern name, circa 1890. *Courtesy of Linda Machalski, L. G. Antiques, Hartley, Delaware.*

BEAUFORT Oval Vegetable Bowl, 1903, by W. H. Grindley & Company, 9 7/8" x 7 1/4". *Courtesy of Louise and Charles Loehr, Louise's Old Things, Kutztown, Pennsylvania.* $125+

W. H. Grindley & Company Ltd., Tunstall, Staffordshire, England, printed globe and ship mark surrounded by banners with manufacturer's name in the lower banner and BEAUFORT pattern name in the upper banner, circa 1891 - 1914. The registration number code indicates the year of pattern registry as 1903. *Courtesy of Louise and Charles Loehr, Louise's Old Things, Kutztown, Pennsylvania.*

BELL Plate, circa 1912, by T. Rathbone & Company, 9 1/4" in diameter. *Courtesy of Louise and Charles Loehr, Louise's Old Things, Kutztown, Pennsylvania.* $35-55

T. Rathbone & Company, Tunstall, Staffordshire, England, printed swan and banner mark with manufacturer's initials (T R & Co.) and BELL pattern name within the banner. Letters are found beneath the manufacturer's name on occasion, as illustrated here, and indicate the potting towns where ceramics were produced. The T beneath the T R & Co. indicates the plate was produced in Tunstall. The major potting towns in England are Burslem (B), Cobridge (C), Fenton (F), Hanley (H), Longton (L) and Tunstall (T). This mark dates from circa 1912. *Courtesy of Louise and Charles Loehr, Louise's Old Things, Kutztown, Pennsylvania.*

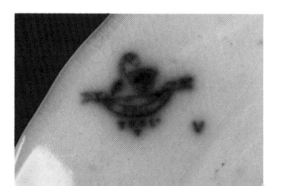

BENTICK Cup, 1905, by Cauldon Ltd., 2 1/2" tall x 3 3/8" in diameter. This cup has an interesting open work handle. *Courtesy of Louise and Charles Loehr, Louise's Old Things, Kutztown, Pennsylvania.* $50+

Cauldon Ltd., Hanley, Staffordshire, England, printed manufacturer's name, no printed or impressed pattern name, 1905 - 1920. *Courtesy of Louise and Charles Loehr, Louise's Old Things, Kutztown, Pennsylvania.*

BLENHEIM Soup Bowl, circa 1919, by Till & Sons, 9" in diameter. *Courtesy of Linda Machalski, L. G. Antiques, Hartley, Delaware.* $50+

Till & Sons, Burslem, Staffordshire, England, printed globe mark with manufacturer's name and BLENHEIM pattern name, circa 1919. *Courtesy of Linda Machalski, L. G. Antiques, Hartley, Delaware.*

THE BLUE DANUBE Gravy Boat, circa 1900 - 1912, by Johnson Bros. Ltd., 7" x 3" x 4". *Courtesy of Louise and Charles Loehr, Louise's Old Things, Kutztown, Pennsylvania.* $150+

Johnson Bros. Ltd., Hanley, Staffordshire, England, printed crown mark with manufacturer's name and THE BLUE DANUBE pattern name, circa 1900 - 1912. *Courtesy of Louise and Charles Loehr, Louise's Old Things, Kutztown, Pennsylvania.*

BRUNSWICK Plate, circa 1891, by Wood & Son, without printed or impressed mark or pattern name, 9" in diameter. *Courtesy of John and Nancy Harner, Dover Antique Mart, Smyrna, Delaware.* $50+

CAMBRIDGE Plate, circa 1890 - 1894, by New Wharf Pottery Company, 9" in diameter. Courtesy of Linda Machalski, L. G. Antiques, Hartley, Delaware. $75+

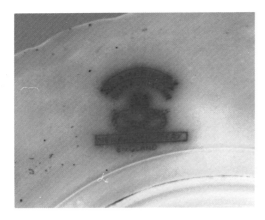

New Wharf Pottery Company, Burslem, Staffordshire, England, printed Staffordshire knot and crown mark with manufacturer's name below the knot and CAMBRIDGE pattern name in a banner above the crown, circa 1890 - 1894. *Courtesy of Linda Machalski, L. G. Antiques, Hartley, Delaware.*

CANDIA Syrup Pitcher, 1900, by Cauldon Ltd., 4 1/2" tall. Two small holes are located on either side of the handle where a lid was once attached. One is visible in the photograph. *Courtesy of Louise and Charles Loehr, Louise's Old Things, Kutztown, Pennsylvania.* $100

CARLSBAD Plate, circa 1895 - 1917, imported by Lewis Straus & Sons, 9 1/2" in diameter. This piece was imported for the American market from Austria. *Courtesy of Linda Machalski, L. G. Antiques, Hartley, Delaware.* $35+

Lewis Straus & Sons, New York, New York, printed circular mark. Lewis Straus & Sons were porcelain importers; it is their initials which appear within the mark along with the CARLSBAD pattern name. The piece originated in Austria but the manufacturer is unknown. Mark dates from circa 1895 to 1917. *Courtesy of Linda Machalski, L. G. Antiques, Hartley, Delaware.*

Cauldon Ltd., Hanley, Staffordshire, England, printed oval banner mark with manufacturer's name beneath and CANDIA pattern name, 1905 - 1920. *Courtesy of Louise and Charles Loehr, Louise's Old Things, Kutztown, Pennsylvania.*

CLARENCE Platter, circa 1891 - 1914, by W. H. Grindley & Company, 12" x 10".
Courtesy of John and Nancy Harner, Dover Antique Mart, Smyrna, Delaware. $125+

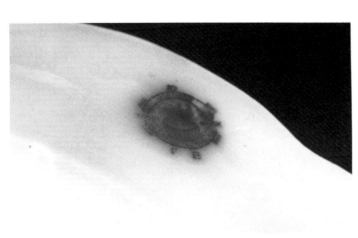

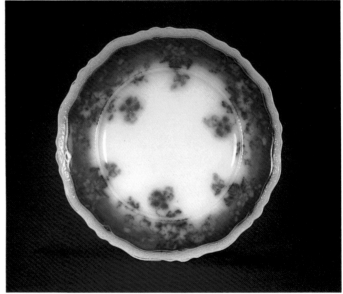

W. H. Grindley & Company Ltd., Tunstall, Staffordshire, England, printed globe and ship mark surrounded by banners with manufacturer's name in the lower banner and CLARENCE pattern name in the upper banner, circa 1891 - 1914. *Courtesy of John and Nancy Harner, Dover Antique Mart, Smyrna, Delaware.*

CLAYTON Plate, circa 1902, by Johnson Bros. Ltd., 9" in diameter. *Courtesy of Marion Butz, The Antique Marketplace, Lancaster, Pennsylvania.* $65-75

Johnson Bros. Ltd., Hanley, Staffordshire, England, printed crown mark with manufacturer's name and CLAYTON pattern name. The patent mark dates the pattern to October 24,1902. *Courtesy of Marion Butz, The Antique Marketplace, Lancaster, Pennsylvania.*

Johnson Bros. Ltd., Hanley, Staffordshire, England, printed crown mark with manufacturer's name and CLAYTON pattern name. The patent mark dates the pattern to October 24,1902. *Courtesy of Marion Butz, The Antique Marketplace, Lancaster, Pennsylvania.*

CLAYTON Butter Pat, circa 1902, by Johnson Bros. Ltd.with no printed or impressed mark or pattern name, 3" in diameter. *Courtesy of Marion Butz, The Antique Marketplace, Lancaster, Pennsylvania.* $30-40

CLAYTON Bowl, circa 1902, by Johnson Bros. Ltd., 7 1/2" in diameter. *Courtesy of Marion Butz, The Antique Marketplace, Lancaster, Pennsylvania.* $50+

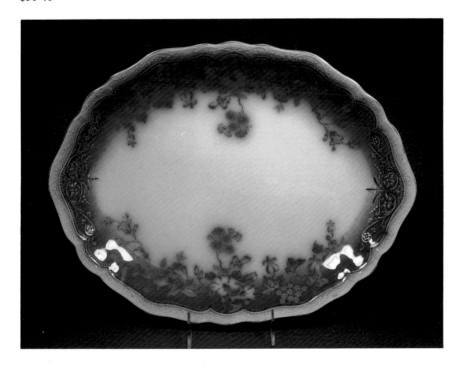

CLAYTON Platter, circa 1902, by Johnson Bros. Ltd., 16 1/4" x 12". Courtesy of Marion Butz, The Antique Marketplace, Lancaster, Pennsylvania. $175+

Johnson Bros. Ltd., Hanley, Staffordshire, England, printed crown mark with manufacturer's name and CLAYTON pattern name. The patent mark dates the pattern to October 24,1902. *Courtesy of Marion Butz, The Antique Marketplace, Lancaster, Pennsylvania.*

CLAYTON Cup and Saucer, 1902, by Johnson Bros. Ltd. The cup measures 2 1/2" tall x 3 1/2" in diameter. The saucer measures 6" in diameter. *Courtesy of Marion Butz, The Antique Marketplace, Lancaster, Pennsylvania.* $75+

CLAYTON Covered Vegetable Dish, circa 1902, by Johnson Bros. Ltd., 6 1/2" tall x 11 1/2". *Courtesy of Marion Butz, The Antique Marketplace, Lancaster, Pennsylvania.* $250-300

CLAYTON Cup and Saucer, 1902, by Johnson Bros. Ltd. The cup measures 2 1/2" tall x 3 1/2" in diameter. The saucer measures 6" in diameter. *Courtesy of Marion Butz, The Antique Marketplace, Lancaster, Pennsylvania.* $75+

Johnson Bros. Ltd., Hanley, Staffordshire, England, printed crown mark with manufacturer's name and CLAYTON pattern name. The patent mark dates the pattern to October 24,1902. *Courtesy of Marion Butz, The Antique Marketplace, Lancaster, Pennsylvania.*

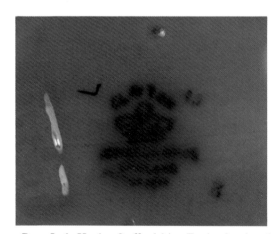

Johnson Bros. Ltd., Hanley, Staffordshire, England, printed crown mark with manufacturer's name and CLAYTON pattern name. The patent mark dates the pattern to October 24,1902. *Courtesy of Marion Butz, The Antique Marketplace, Lancaster, Pennsylvania.*

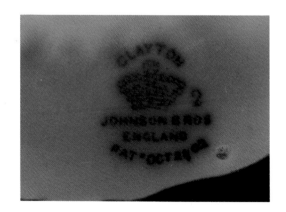

CLIFTON Vegetable Bowl, circa 1891 - 1914, by W. H. Grindley & Company, 9" x 7". *Courtesy of Linda Machalski, L. G. Antiques, Hartley, Delaware.* $100+

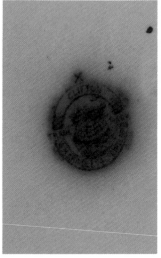

W. H. Grindley & Company Ltd., Tunstall, Staffordshire, England, printed globe and ship mark surrounded by banners with manufacturer's name in the lower banner and CLIFTON pattern name in the upper banner, circa 1891 - 1914. *Courtesy of Linda Machalski, L. G. Antiques, Hartley, Delaware.*

COLONIAL Relish Dish or Gravy Underplate, circa 1907, by J. & G. Meakin, 8 3/8". *Courtesy of Louise and Charles Loehr, Louise's Old Things, Kutztown, Pennsylvania.* $75+

J. & G. Meakin (Ltd.), Hanley, Staffordshire, England, printed crown and circle mark with manufacturer's name across the center of the circle and COLONIAL pattern name above the mark, circa 1907. *Courtesy of Louise and Charles Loehr, Louise's Old Things, Kutztown, Pennsylvania.*

CONWAY Plate, circa 1890 - 1894, by New Wharf Pottery Company, 10 1/2" in diameter. *Courtesy of Bonne Hohl.* $90+

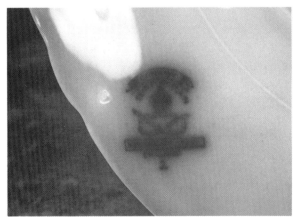

New Wharf Pottery Company, Burslem, Staffordshire, England, printed Staffordshire knot and crown mark with manufacturer's name below the knot and CONWAY pattern name in a banner above the crown, circa 1890 - 1894. *Courtesy of Bonne Hohl.*

CONWAY Covered Vegetable Dish, circa 1891 - 1907, Wood & Son, 6 1/2" tall x 11 1/2". This is a rare piece. Courtesy of Bonne Hohl. $250+

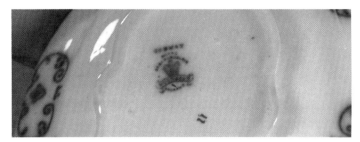

Wood & Son(s Ltd.), Burslem, Staffordshire, England, printed crown mark with mark within a banner beneath the crown and CONWAY pattern name above the crown mark. This mark dates from 1891 - 1907. *Courtesy of Bonne Hohl.*

CORINTHIAN FLUTE Butter Pat, 1905, by Cauldon Ltd., 3 1/2" in diameter. *Courtesy of Louise and Charles Loehr, Louise's Old Things, Kutztown, Pennsylvania.* $30-40

CONWAY Cream Pitcher, circa 1878 - 1894, by New Wharf Pottery Company, 3 1/2" tall. *Courtesy of John and Nancy Harner, Dover Antique Mart, Smyrna, Delaware.* $175+

Cauldon Ltd., Hanley, Staffordshire, England, printed and impressed manufacturer's name, no printed or impressed pattern name, 1905 - 1920. *Courtesy of Louise and Charles Loehr, Louise's Old Things, Kutztown, Pennsylvania.*

CRAWFORD Pitcher, 1891, by Upper Hanley Pottery Company, 5" tall. This is a small advertising pitcher for Crawford Cooking Ranges. These were fairly common pieces. *Courtesy of Louise and Charles Loehr, Louise's Old Things, Kutztown, Pennsylvania.* $150+

New Wharf Pottery Company, Burslem, Staffordshire, England, printed manufacturer's name and CONWAY pattern name, circa 1878 - 1894. *Courtesy of John and Nancy Harner, Dover Antique Mart, Smyrna, Delaware.*

Upper Hanley Pottery Company, Cobridge, Staffordshire, England, printed crown and circle mark with manufacturer's name, no pattern mark, 1895 - 1910. *Courtesy of Louise and Charles Loehr, Louise's Old Things, Kutztown, Pennsylvania.*

CYPRESS Pitcher with 8 side panels, 1898, by Samuel Ford & Company, 7 1/2" tall. It is important to be aware that some Oriental influence remains in the Late Victorian period. This piece even has the side panels seen in earlier pieces. Be sure to check the mark whenever possible. *Courtesy of Louise and Charles Loehr, Louise's Old Things, Kutztown, Pennsylvania.* $150+

CROXTON Sauce Tureen with Slotted Lid and Ladle, 1912, by Keeling & Company Ltd. The tureen measures 4 1/2" tall x 5" in diameter and the ladle measures 7" in length. The finial is a flower bud with embossed leaves surrounding it. *Courtesy of Louise and Charles Loehr, Louise's Old Things, Kutztown, Pennsylvania.* $175+

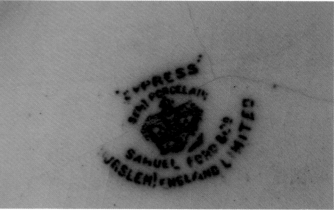

Samuel Ford & Company, Burslem, Staffordshire, England, printed crown mark with manufacturer's name and CYPRESS pattern name, 1898 - 1939. *Courtesy of Louise and Charles Loehr, Louise's Old Things, Kutztown, Pennsylvania.*

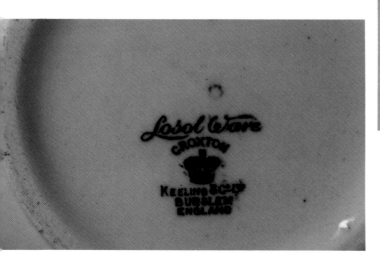

Keeling & Company Ltd., Burslem, Staffordshire, England, printed crown mark with manufacturer's name and CROXTON pattern name, circa 1912 - 1936. *Courtesy of Louise and Charles Loehr, Louise's Old Things, Kutztown, Pennsylvania.*

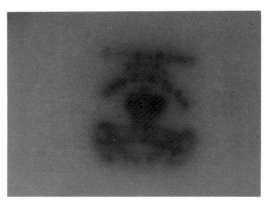

Wood & Sons, Burslem, Staffordshire, England, printed crown & banner mark with manufacturer's name in banner and DAVENPORT pattern name above the mark, circa 1907 - 1910. "Ltd." added to manufacturer's name circa 1910. *Courtesy of Louise and Charles Loehr, Louise's Old Things, Kutztown, Pennsylvania.*

DAINTY Covered Vegetable Dish, circa 1896, by John Maddock & Son, 9 1/2" x 6" x 6". *Courtesy of Linda Machalski, L. G. Antiques, Hartley, Delaware.* $200+

John Maddock & Sons Ltd., Burslem, Staffordshire, England, printed crown and circle mark with manufacturer's name below the crown and DAINTY pattern name beneath the mark, circa 1896. *Courtesy of Linda Machalski, L. G. Antiques, Hartley, Delaware.*

DAVENPORT Covered Vegetable Dish, circa 1907, by Wood & Sons, 9 1/2" x 7 1/2" x 4 1/2". *Courtesy of Louise and Charles Loehr, Louise's Old Things, Kutztown, Pennsylvania.* $200+

DELAMERE Covered Vegetable Dish, 1880 - 1910, by Henry Alcock & Company, 9 1/4" x 7 1/2" x 4". *Courtesy of Louise and Charles Loehr, Louise's Old Things, Kutztown, Pennsylvania.* $250-350

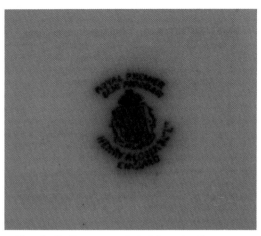

Henry Alcock & Company, Cobridge, Staffordshire, England, printed crown and shield mark with manufacturer's name, no pattern name, 1880 - 1910. *Courtesy of Louise and Charles Loehr, Louise's Old Things, Kutztown, Pennsylvania.*

Globe Pottery Company Ltd., Cobridge, Staffordshire, England, printed crown and globe mark with manufacturer's name in a banner across the center of the mark and DELPH pattern name above the mark. *Courtesy of Marion Butz, The Antique Marketplace, Lancaster, Pennsylvania.*

DELPH Plate, 1917, by Globe Pottery Company Ltd., 10" in diameter. This pattern is similar to a MADRAS pattern by Upper Hanley Pottery. *Courtesy of Marion Butz, The Antique Marketplace, Lancaster, Pennsylvania.* $40-60

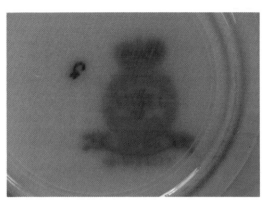

E. Bourne & J. E. Leigh, Burslem, Staffordshire, England, printed crown and circle mark with manufacturer's initials (ERJEL) and DELPH pattern name in a banner beneath the mark, circa 1892 - 1939. *Courtesy of Marion Butz, The Antique Marketplace, Lancaster, Pennsylvania.*

DELPH Bowl, circa 1892, by E. Bourne & J.E. Leigh, 10 3/8" in diameter. This pattern is similar to a MADRAS pattern by Upper Hanley Pottery. *Courtesy of Marion Butz, The Anitque Marketplace, Lancaster, Pennslyvania.* $110+

DORIS Covered Vegetable Dish, 1891, by W. H. Grindley & Company, 10" x 8 1/2" x 6". *Courtesy of Louise and Charles Loehr, Louise's Old Things, Kutztown, Pennsylvania.* $200+

W. H. Grindley & Company Ltd., Tunstall, Staffordshire, England, printed globe and ship mark surrounded by banners with manufacturer's name in the lower banner and DORIS pattern name in the upper banner, circa 1891 - 1914. *Courtesy of Louise and Charles Loehr, Louise's Old Things, Kutztown, Pennsylvania.*

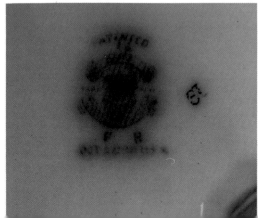

DOROTHY Luncheon Set (one place setting and tea service), circa 1900 - 1904, by W. & E. Corn. From left to right and back to front: honey dish, 5" in diameter; luncheon plate, 9" in diameter; salad plate, 8" in diameter; sugar bowl with two handles, 6" tall x 4 1/2" in diameter; cream pitcher, 5" tall; teapot, 7" tall; tea cup and saucer, the cup measures 2 1/4" tall x 3 1/4" in diameter and the saucer measures 5 1/2" in diameter. The waste bowl in the following photograph would also have been common to this set. *Courtesy of Jacqueline Hunsicker.* $800-1000

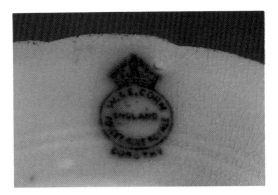

W. & E. Corn, Longport, Staffordshire, England, printed crown and circle mark with manufacturer's name and DOROTHY pattern name, circa 1900 - 1904. *Courtesy of Jacqueline Hunsicker.*

DOROTHY Waste Bowl, circa 1900 - 1904, by W. & E. Corn, 3 1/2" tall x 6" in diameter. *Courtesy of Jacqueline Hunsicker.* $150

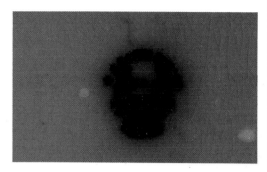

W. & E. Corn, Longport, Staffordshire, England, printed laurel mark with manufacturer's name over the mark and DOROTHY pattern name below, circa 1900 - 1904. *Courtesy of Jacqueline Hunsicker.*

DRESDEN Platter, circa 1900, by Villeroy & Boch, 14" x 10 1/4". *Courtesy of Louise and Charles Loehr, Louise's Old Things, Kutztown, Pennsylvania.* $100+

DOROTHY Compote, 1897, by W. H. Grindley & Company, 10" x 9" x 4 1/4". This is a significantly different pattern design from W. & E. Corn's DOROTHY. *Courtesy of John and Nancy Harner, Dover Antique Mart, Smyrna, Delaware.* $100+

W. H. Grindley & Company Ltd., Tunstall, Staffordshire, England, printed globe and ship mark surrounded by banners with manufacturer's name in the lower banner and DOROTHY pattern name in the upper banner, circa 1891 - 1914. This is an unusually clear Grindley mark. *Courtesy of John and Nancy Harner, Dover Antique Mart, Smyrna, Delaware.*

Villeroy & Boch, Mettlach Saar, Germany, printed mark with manufacturer's name, no pattern name, 1874 - present. *Courtesy of Louise and Charles Loehr, Louise's Old Things, Kutztown, Pennsylvania.*

DUCHESS Platter, 1891, by W. H. Grindley & Company, 15 3/4" x 11". *Courtesy of John and Nancy Harner, Dover Antique Mart, Smyrna, Delaware.* $150+

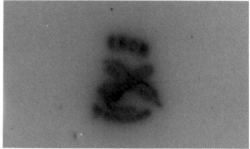

Ridgways, Hanley, Staffordshire, England, printed bow and arrow mark with manufacturer's name within the arrow and EBOR pattern name above the mark, 1912 - 1920. *Courtesy of Louise and Charles Loehr, Louise's Old Things, Kutztown, Pennsylvania.*

W. H. Grindley & Company Ltd., Tunstall, Staffordshire, England, printed globe and ship mark surrounded by banners with manufacturer's name in the lower banner and DUCHESS pattern name in the upper banner, circa 1891 - 1914. The registration number (Rd. No.) code indicates a registry date of 1891. *Courtesy of John and Nancy Harner, Dover Antique Mart, Smyrna, Delaware.*

EDGAR Plate, circa 1890 - 1894, by New Wharf Pottery Company, 9" in diameter. *Courtesy of Linda Machalski, L. G. Antiques, Hartley, Delaware.* $50+

EBOR Oval Vegetable Bowl (lid missing), 1912, by Ridgways, 3" tall x 12" in length. *Courtesy of Louise and Charles Loehr, Louise's Old Things, Kutztown, Pennsylvania.* $75+

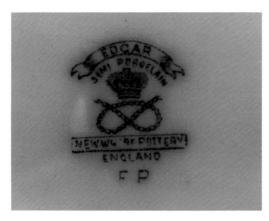

New Wharf Pottery Company, Burslem, Staffordshire, England, printed Staffordshire knot and crown mark with manufacturer's name below the knot and EDGAR pattern name in a banner above the crown, circa 1890 - 1894. *Courtesy of Linda Machalski, L. G. Antiques, Hartley, Delaware.*

FISH Sauce Boat, circa 1905, by Cauldon Ltd., 7" x 2 7/8" x 4 1/4". *Courtesy of Louise and Charles Loehr, Louise's Old Things, Kutztown, Pennsylvania.* $125

Cauldon Ltd., Hanley, Staffordshire, England, printed manufacturer's name, no printed or impressed pattern name, 1905 - 1920. *Courtesy of Louise and Charles Loehr, Louise's Old Things, Kutztown, Pennsylvania.*

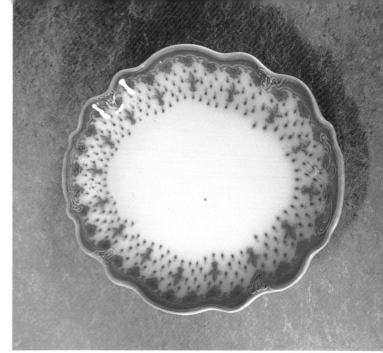

FLEUR-DE-LIS Platter, circa 1907, by J. & G. Meakin Ltd., 18" x 14". *Courtesy of Linda Machalski, L. G. Antiques, Hartley, Delaware.* $175-250

FLEUR-DE-LIS Platter, circa 1907, by J. & G. Meakin, 18" x 14". A closer look at this large platter. *Courtesy of Linda Machalski, L. G. Antiques, Hartley, Delaware.* $175-250

J. & G. Meakin (Ltd.), Hanley, Staffordshire, England, printed crown and circle mark with manufacturer's name and "FLEUR DE LIS" pattern name, circa 1907. *Courtesy of Linda Machalski, L. G. Antiques, Hartley, Delaware.*

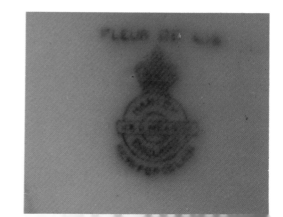

FLORIDA Platter, circa 1900, by Johnson Bros., 10 1/2" x 7" x 2 1/2". *Courtesy of John and Nancy Harner, Dover Antique Mart, Smyrna, Delaware.* $75+

Johnson Bros. Ltd., Hanley & Tunstall, Staffordshire, England, printed crown and banner mark with manufacturer's name within the banner and FLORIDA pattern name above the crown, circa 1900. *Courtesy of John and Nancy Harner, Dover Antique Mart, Smyrna, Delaware.*

GEISHA Plate, 1893, by Ford and Sons, 9 1/2" in diameter. The sides slope slightly upward suggesting this may be a cake plate. *Courtesy of Louise and Charles Loehr, Louise's Old Things, Kutztown, Pennsylvania.* $50+

Ford & Sons (Ltd.), Burslem, Staffordshire, England, printed banner mark with F. & SONS manufacturer's name above the mark and GEISHA pattern name within the banner mark, 1893 - 1938. *Courtesy of Louise and Charles Loehr, Louise's Old Things, Kutztown, Pennsylvania.*

GIBSON WIDOW Plate, circa 1902, Doulton & Company, 10 1/2" in diameter. The central scene is in black and the inscription at its base reads "She Goes To The Fancy Dress Ball As 'Juliet.'" *Courtesy of Louise and Charles Loehr, Louise's Old Things, Kutztown, Pennsylvania.* $155-175

GEORGIA Platter, circa 1913, by Johnson Bros., 16" x 12". This pattern makes striking use of the white open space of the platter to create a complimentary six point star pattern. *Courtesy of Linda Machalski, L. G. Antiques, Hartley, Delaware.* $275+

Doulton & Company (Ltd.), Burslem, Staffordshire, England, printed crown and circle mark with Royal Doulton manufacturer's name within the circle, no pattern name, circa 1902 - 1930. "Made in England" was added to the mark in 1930. *Courtesy of Louise and Charles Loehr, Louise's Old Things, Kutztown, Pennsylvania.*

Johnson Bros. Ltd., Hanley, Staffordshire, England, printed crown mark with manufacturer's name and GEORGIA pattern name, circa 1900. *Courtesy of Linda Machalski, L. G. Antiques, Hartley, Delaware.*

GLADYS Platter, circa 1891, by New Wharf Pottery Company, 10 3/4" x 9". *Courtesy of Linda Machalski, L. G. Antiques, Hartley, Delaware.* $85-110

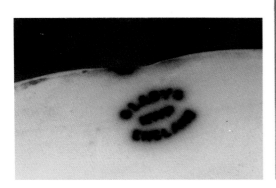

New Wharf Pottery Company, Burslem, Staffordshire, England, printed manufacturer's initials and GLADYS pattern name, circa 1878 - 1894. *Courtesy of Linda Machalski, L. G. Antiques, Hartley, Delaware.*

GRACE Gravy Underplate, circa 1897, by W. H. Grindley & Company, 9 1/2" x 6 1/2". *Courtesy of Linda Machalski, L. G. Antiques, Hartley, Delaware.* $125

W. H. Grindley & Company Ltd., Tunstall, Staffordshire, England, printed globe and ship mark surrounded by banners with manufacturer's name in the lower banner and GRACE pattern name in the upper banner, circa 1891 - 1914. The registration number code indicates the year of pattern registry as 1897. *Courtesy of Linda Machalski, L. G. Antiques, Hartley, Delaware.*

HOLLAND Plate, 1891, by Johnson Bros., 10" in diameter. *Courtesy of Louise and Charles Loehr, Louise's Old Things, Kutztown, Pennsylvania.* $125

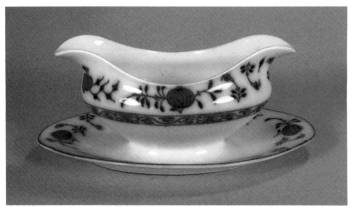

HOLLAND Gravy Boat with attached underplate, 1891, by Johnson Bros., 9" x 5 1/2" x 3 3/4". *Courtesy of Louise and Charles Loehr, Louise's Old Things, Kutztown, Pennsylvania.* $275-350

HOLLAND Cup and Saucer, 1891, by Johnson Bros. The cup measures 2 1/4" tall x 3 5/8" in diameter. The saucer measures 6" in diameter. *Courtesy of Louise and Charles Loehr, Louise's Old Things, Kutztown, Pennsylvania.* $90-110

Johnson Bros. Ltd., Hanley, Staffordshire, England, printed crown mark with manufacturer's name and HOLLAND pattern name, circa 1900. *Courtesy of Louise and Charles Loehr, Louise's Old Things, Kutztown, Pennsylvania.*

HONC Pedestal Bowl, circa 1900, by Petrus Regout, 3 1/4" tall x 5 1/4" in diameter. Courtesy of Louise and Charles Loehr, Louise's Old Things, Kutztown, Pennsylvania. $100+

HOMESTEAD Butter Pat, 1907, by J. & G. Meakin, 3" in diameter. On a larger piece it would be easier to see that the central design portrays a country home. The border pattern continues the motif in part with three different farm houses and surrounding rural landscapes. Between the scenes around the border are scroll and floral designs. *Courtesy of Louise and Charles Loehr, Louise's Old Things, Kutztown, Pennsylvania.* $30-40

J. & G. Meakin (Ltd.), Hanley, Staffordshire, England, printed crown and circle mark with manufacturer's name across the center of the circle and HOMESTEAD pattern name above the mark, circa 1907. *Courtesy of Louise and Charles Loehr, Louise's Old Things, Kutztown, Pennsylvania.*

Petrus Regout & Company, Maastricht, Holland, printed sphinx mark with manufacturer's name and HONC pattern name. *Courtesy of Louise and Charles Loehr, Louise's Old Things, Kutztown, Pennsylvania.*

IVANHOE Plate, circa 1901, by Josiah Wedgwood, 10 1/4" in diameter. At the feet of the central figures is printed "Rebecca Repelling the Templar." Courtesy of Bonne Hohl. $125+

IDRIS Plate, circa 1914 - 1925, by W. H. Grindley & Company, 9" in diameter. *Courtesy of Linda Machalski, L. G. Antiques, Hartley, Delaware.* $50+

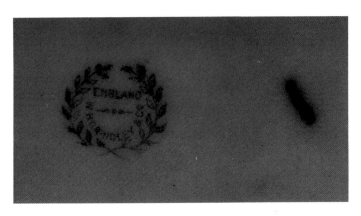

IVANHOE Plate, circa 1901, by Josiah Wedgwood, 10 1/4" in diameter. Beside Rebecca's right leg is printed "Ivanhoe and Rowena." There are a series of these IVANHOE plates with other scenes and emotions to collect. *Courtesy of Bonne Hohl.* $125+

W. H. Grindley & Company Ltd., Tunstall, Staffordshire, England, printed mark with manufacturer's name in a separate color and IDRIS pattern name off to one side, circa 1914 - 1925. *Courtesy of Linda Machalski, L. G. Antiques, Hartley, Delaware.*

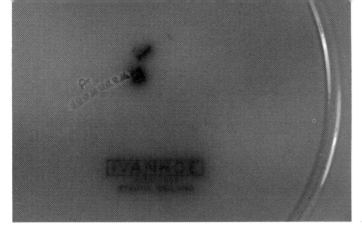

Josiah Wedgwood (& Sons Ltd.), Etruria, England, printed and impressed manufacturer's name and IVANHOE pattern name. *Courtesy of Bonne Hohl.*

KYBER Platter, 1893 - 1917, by William Adams & Company, 10" x 7 1/2". *Courtesy of Linda Machalski, L. G. Antiques, Hartley, Delaware.* $125

KNOX Plate, circa 1890 - 1894, by New Wharf Pottery Company, 7" in diameter. *Courtesy of Linda Machalski, L. G. Antiques, Hartley, Delaware.* $50+

William Adams & Company, Tunstall and Stoke, Staffordshire, England, printed mark with manufacturer's name and KYBER pattern name, 1893 - 1917. *Courtesy of Linda Machalski, L. G. Antiques, Hartley, Delaware.*

New Wharf Pottery Company, Burslem, Staffordshire, England, printed Staffordshire knot and crown mark with manufacturer's name below the knot and KNOX pattern name in a banner above the crown, circa 1890 - 1894. *Courtesy of Linda Machalski, L. G. Antiques, Hartley, Delaware.*

French China, East Liverpool, Ohio, printed mark, no manufacturer's name and LA FRANCAISE pattern name, 1916 - 1929. *Courtesy of Louise and Charles Loehr, Louise's Old Things, Kutztown, Pennsylvania.*

LA BELLE Bowl, 1893, by Wheeling Pottery Company, 5 1/2" in diameter. *Courtesy of John and Nancy Harner, Dover Antique Mart, Smyrna, Delaware.* $100

Wheeling Pottery Company, Wheeling, West Virginia, printed mark with manufacturer's initials (WP) and LA BELLE pattern name, 1893. *Courtesy of John and Nancy Harner, Dover Antique Mart, Smyrna, Delaware.*

LA FRANCAISE Covered Butter Dish with Insert, circa 1916 - 1922, by French China, 7 1/2" tall. *Courtesy of Louise and Charles Loehr, Louise's Old Things, Kutztown, Pennsylvania.* $75-95

LADAS Platter, circa 1905 - 1920, by Ridgways, 16" x 12". *Courtesy of Linda Machalski, L. G. Antiques, Hartley, Delaware.* $125-175

Ridgways, Hanley, Staffordshire, England, printed crown and circle mark with manufacturer's name directly beneath the crown and LADAS pattern name below the circle, circa 1905 - 1920. *Courtesy of Linda Machalski, L. G. Antiques, Hartley, Delaware.*

LAHORE Plate, circa 1900, by W. & E. Corn, 8 5/8" in diameter. *Courtesy of Louise and Charles Loehr, Louise's Old Things, Kutztown, Pennsylvania.* $75+

W. & E. Corn, Longport, Staffordshire, England, no printed or impressed mark, printed LAHORE pattern name, 1864 - 1900. Prior to 1900 most W. & E. Corn pieces were left without marks. *Courtesy of Louise and Charles Loehr, Louise's Old Things, Kutztown, Pennsylvania.*

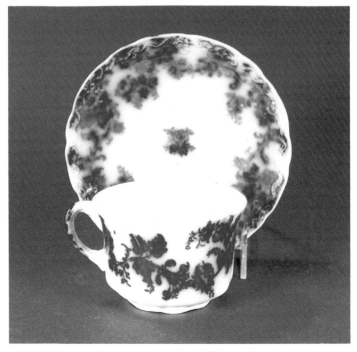

LANCASTER Cup and Saucer, circa 1891, no printed or impressed mark for identification of the manufacturer. The cup measures 2 1/4" tall x 3 5/8" in diameter and the saucer measures 6" in diameter. *Courtesy of John and Nancy Harner, Dover Antique Mart, Smyrna, Delaware.* $85-110

LANCASTER printed pattern name without printed or impressed mark, circa 1891. *Courtesy of John and Nancy Harner, Dover Antique Mart, Smyrna, Delaware.*

LAWRENCE Butter Pat, 1899, by Bishop & Stonier, 3" in diameter. *Courtesy of Louise and Charles Loehr, Louise's Old Things, Kutztown, Pennsylvania.* $30-40

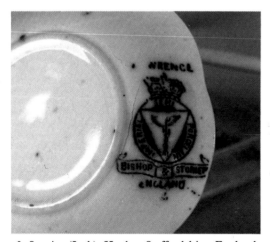

Bishop & Stonier (Ltd.), Hanley, Staffordshire, England, printed crown and circle mark with manufacturer's name in a banner beneath and LAWRENCE pattern name above the crown, 1899 - 1936. *Courtesy of Louise and Charles Loehr, Louise's Old Things, Kutztown, Pennsylvania.*

LEICESTER Soup Bowl, 1906, by Sampson Hancock, 7 3/4" in diameter. *Courtesy of Louise and Charles Loehr, Louise's Old Things, Kutztown, Pennsylvania.* $60+

Sampson Hancock & Sons, Stoke, Staffordshire, England, printed crown mark with manufacturers initials (SH & S) beneath and LEICESTER pattern name above, 1906 - 1912. *Courtesy of Louise and Charles Loehr, Louise's Old Things, Kutztown, Pennsylvania.*

LEON Berry/Dessert Bowl, 1891, by J. & G. Meakin, 5 1/4" in diameter. *Courtesy of Louise and Charles Loehr, Louise's Old Things, Kutztown, Pennsylvania.* $40+

J. & G. Meakin (Ltd.), Hanley, Staffordshire, England, printed manufacturer's name and LEON pattern name, 1891. *Courtesy of Louise and Charles Loehr, Louise's Old Things, Kutztown, Pennsylvania.*

John Maddock & Sons Ltd., Burslem, Staffordshire, England, printed crown and circle mark with manufacturer's name below the crown and LINDA pattern name beneath the mark, circa 1896. *Courtesy of Linda Machalski, L. G. Antiques, Hartley, Delaware.*

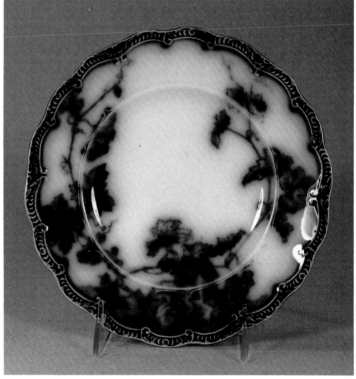

LEON Cup and Saucer, 1891, by J. & G. Meakin. The cup measures 2 1/2" tall x 3 1/2" in diameter and the saucer measures 5 7/8" in diameter. *Courtesy of Louise and Charles Loehr, Louise's Old Things, Kutztown, Pennsylvania.* $80-100

LINDA Cream Pitcher, circa 1896, by John Maddock & Sons, 4 1/2" tall. *Courtesy of Linda Machalski, L. G. Antiques, Hartley, Delaware.* $125+

LONSDALE Plate, circa 1912, by Ridgways, 8" in diameter. *Courtesy of Linda Machalski, L. G. Antiques, Hartley, Delaware.* $50

Ridgways, Hanley, Staffordshire, England, printed bow and arrow mark with manufacturer's name within the arrow and LONSDALE pattern name above the mark, 1912 - 1920. *Courtesy of Linda Machalski, L. G. Antiques, Hartley, Delaware.*

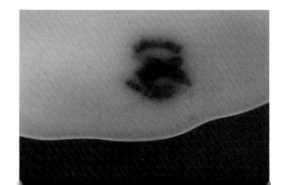

LORNE Platter, circa 1900, by W. H. Grindley & Company, 16" x 12". *Courtesy of Louise and Charles Loehr, Louise's Old Things, Kutztown, Pennsylvania.* $250-285

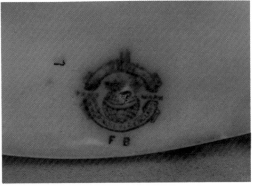

W. H. Grindley & Company Ltd., Tunstall, Staffordshire, England, printed globe and ship mark surrounded by banners with manufacturer's name in the lower banner and LORNE pattern name in the upper banner, circa 1891 - 1914. *Courtesy of Louise and Charles Loehr, Louise's Old Things, Kutztown, Pennsylvania.*

LORRAINE Oval Individual Vegetable Bowl, 1905, by Ridgways, 5 3/4" x 4 1/4". *Courtesy of Louise and Charles Loehr, Louise's Old Things, Kutztown, Pennsylvania.* $60+

Ridgways, Hanley, Staffordshire, England, printed crown and circle mark with manufacturer's name directly beneath crown and LORRAINE pattern name beneath the circle, circa 1905. *Courtesy of Louise and Charles Loehr, Louise's Old Things, Kutztown, Pennsylvania.*

LUCERNE Gravy Underplate, circa 1891, by F. Winkle & Company, 8 1/2" x 4 3/4". *Courtesy of Louise and Charles Loehr, Louise's Old Things, Kutztown, Pennsylvania.* $75+

F. Winkle & Company, Stoke, Staffordshire, England, printed manufacturer's initials and LUCERNE pattern name, 1890 - 1931. *Courtesy of Louise and Charles Loehr, Louise's Old Things, Kutztown, Pennsylvania.*

LUNEVILLE Plate, circa 1900, unidentified French potter, 8 3/4" in diameter. *Courtesy of Louise and Charles Loehr, Louise's Old Things, Kutztown, Pennsylvania.* $30+

LUSITANIA Vegetable Bowl, 1891, by Wood & Son, 9 3/4" in diameter. *Courtesy of Louise and Charles Loehr, Louise's Old Things, Kutztown, Pennsylvania.* $75+

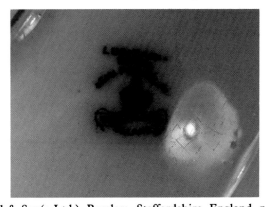

Wood & Son(s Ltd.), Burslem, Staffordshire, England, printed crown and banner mark with manufacturer's name in the banner and LUSITANIA pattern name above the mark, 1891 - 1907. *Courtesy of Louise and Charles Loehr, Louise's Old Things, Kutztown, Pennsylvania.*

Unidentified printed crown and crest mark, France, and LUNEVILLE pattern name beneath the mark, circa 1900. *Courtesy of Louise and Charles Loehr, Louise's Old Things, Kutztown, Pennsylvania.*

LUZERNE Salad Bowl, circa 1902, by Mercer Pottery Company, 6 1/8" in diameter. *Courtesy of Marion Butz, The Antique Marketplace, Lancaster, Pennsylvania.* $40+

LUZERNE Soup Bowl with Rim, circa 1902, by Mercer Pottery Company, 8 3/4" in diameter. *Courtesy of Louise and Charles Loehr, Louise's Old Things, Kutztown, Pennsylvania.* $60-85

Mercer Pottery Company, Trenton, New Jersey, printed crown and shield mark with manufacturer's name across shield, no pattern name, circa 1902. *Courtesy of Marion Butz, The Antique Marketplace, Lancaster, Pennsylvania.*

Mercer Pottery Company, Trenton, New Jersey, printed crown and shield mark with manufacturer's name across shield, no pattern name, circa 1902. *Courtesy of Louise and Charles Loehr, Louise's Old Things, Kutztown, Pennsylvania.*

MADRAS Pitcher, circa 1902 - 1930, by Doulton and Company, 7 5/8" tall. *Courtesy of Louise and Charles Loehr, Louise's Old Things, Kutztown, Pennsylvania.* $275+

MADRAS Plate, circa 1882 - 1902, by Doulton & Company, 9 1/2" in diameter. One of two MADRAS patterns by two potters illustrated here. *Courtesy of Louise and Charles Loehr, Louise's Old Things, Kutztown, Pennsylvania.* $75+

Doulton & Company, Burslem, Staffordshire, England, printed mark with manufacturer's (Royal Doulton) name and MADRAS pattern name, circa 1902 - 1930. *Courtesy of Louise and Charles Loehr, Louise's Old Things, Kutztown, Pennsylvania.*

Doulton & Company (Ltd.), Burslem, Staffordshire, England, printed crown and circle mark with manufacturer's name immediately below crown and MADRAS pattern name below the mark, circa 1882 - 1902. *Courtesy of Louise and Charles Loehr, Louise's Old Things, Kutztown, Pennsylvania.*

MADRAS Platter, 1895 -1910, by Upper Hanley Pottery Company, 15 1/4" x 11 1/2". This alternate MADRAS pattern is very similar to DELPH. *Courtesy of Linda Machalski, L. G. Antiques, Hartley, Delaware.* $175+

Upper Hanley Pottery Company, Hanley & Cobridge, Staffordshire, England, printed crown and circle mark with manufacturer's name below the crown and MADRAS pattern name beneath the circle, 1895 - 1910. *Courtesy of Linda Machalski, L. G. Antiques, Hartley, Delaware.*

MADRAS Sugar Bowl, 1895 - 1910, by Upper Hanley Pottery Company, 6" tall. *Courtesy of Linda Machalski, L. G. Antiques, Hartley, Delaware.* $110+

Upper Hanley Pottery Company, Hanley & Cobridge, Staffordshire, England, printed crown and circle mark with manufacturer's name below the crown and MADRAS pattern name beneath the circle, 1895 - 1910. *Courtesy of Linda Machalski, L. G. Antiques, Hartley, Delaware.*

MANDARIN Two Cup Sauce Tureen with underplate, 1900, by Pountney & Company. The piece measures 5 1/2" tall and the underplate measures 8 7/8" x 6 7/8". The lid is slotted, however, the ladle is missing. This is an uncommon piece. *Courtesy of Louise and Charles Loehr, Louise's Old Things, Kutztown, Pennsylvania.* $150+

MALTA Round Trivet, 1891, by Franz Anton Mehlem Earthenware Factory, 6 7/8" in diameter. *Courtesy of Louise and Charles Loehr, Louise's Old Things, Kutztown, Pennsylvania.* $75+

Pountney & Company (Ltd.), Bristol, Gloucestershire, England, printed triangular mark with central crossed swords and 1750 date of establishment. This does not date the mark, it was in use in circa 1900. The manufacturer's name is in the left side of the triangle and the MANDARIN pattern name is located in the base of the triangle. *Courtesy of Louise and Charles Loehr, Louise's Old Things, Kutztown, Pennsylvania.*

MANHATTAN Tea Cup Saucer, 1880 - 1910, by Henry Alcock & Company, 6" in diameter. *Courtesy of Linda Machalski, L. G. Antiques, Hartley, Delaware.* $30+

Franz Anton Mehlem Earthenware Factory, Bonn, Rhineland, Germany, printed and impressed mark with manufacturer's initials and printed MALTA pattern name, 1891. *Courtesy of Louise and Charles Loehr, Louise's Old Things, Kutztown, Pennsylvania.*

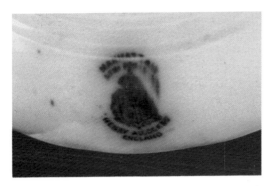

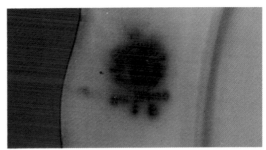

Henry Alcock & Company, Cobridge, Staffordshire, England, printed crown and shield mark with manufacturer's name below the shield and MANHATTAN pattern name above the crown, 1880 - 1910. *Courtesy of Linda Machalski, L. G. Antiques, Hartley, Delaware.*

W. H. Grindley & Company Ltd., Tunstall, Staffordshire, England, printed globe and ship mark surrounded by banners with manufacturer's name in the lower banner and MARECHAL NIEL pattern name in the upper banner, circa 1891 - 1914. The registration number (Rd. No.) indicates the year of registration was 1896. *Courtesy of Linda Machalski, L. G. Antiques, Hartley, Delaware.*

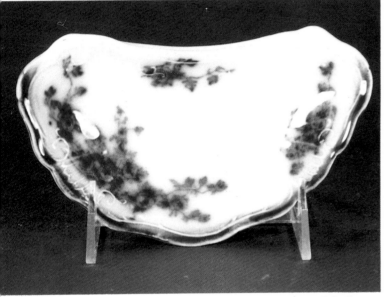

MARECHAL NIEL Bone Dish, circa 1891 - 1914, by W. H. Grindley & Company, 6 1/8" x 3 3/8". *Courtesy of John and Nancy Harner, Dover Antique Mart, Smyrna, Delaware.* $75+

MARIE Butter Dish, 1895, W. H. Grindley & Company, 3 1/2" tall x 7 1/4" in diameter. *Courtesy of Louise and Charles Loehr, Louise's Old Things, Kutztown, Pennsylvania.* $200+

MARECHAL NIEL Relish Dish, 1896, by W. H. Grindley & Company, 9" x 4 1/2". *Courtesy of Linda Machalski, L. G. Antiques, Hartley, Delaware.* $125+

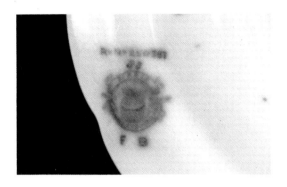

W. H. Grindley & Company Ltd., Tunstall, Staffordshire, England, printed globe and ship mark surrounded by banners with manufacturer's name in the lower banner and MARIE pattern name in the upper banner, circa 1891 - 1914. The registration number (Rd. No.) indicates the year of registration was 1895. *Courtesy of Louise and Charles Loehr, Louise's Old Things, Kutztown, Pennsylvania.*

MARTHA WASHINGTON Plate, 1900, no printed or impressed mark to identify the English potter, 8 3/4" in diameter. This pattern has also been identified with the descriptive name "Chain of States." Courtesy of Louise and Charles Loehr, Louise's Old Things, Kutztown, Pennsylvania. $80-100

MARTHA Bone Dish, 1896, by Bridgett & Bates, 6 1/8" x 3 3/8". Courtesy of Louise and Charles Loehr, Louise's Old Things, Kutztown, Pennsylvania. $60

Unidentified manufacturer of MARTHA WASHINGTON pattern plate. This was produced specifically for the Shawmut Furniture Company, Boston, Massachusetts, 1900. *Courtesy of Louise and Charles Loehr, Louise's Old Things, Kutztown, Pennsylvania.*

Bridgett & Bates, Longton, Staffordshire, England, printed circular mark and MARTHA pattern name below the mark. The registration number (Rd. No.) provides an 1896 date of registry. *Courtesy of Louise and Charles Loehr, Louise's Old Things, Kutztown, Pennsylvania.*

MELBORNE Sugar Bowl, 1900, by W. H. Grindley & Company, 6"
tall. *Courtesy of Louise and Charles Loehr, Louise's Old Things, Kutztown,
Pennsylvania.* $250-325

MARTHA WASHINGTON Cup and Saucer, 1900, no printed or
impressed mark to identify the English potter. The cup measures 2
1/4" tall x 3 1/2" in diameter and the saucer measures 6" in diameter.
An example in Flow Blue of a pattern designed in England specifically for the American market. This is more commonly seen in
unflown transfer printed wares. *Courtesy of Louise and Charles Loehr,
Louise's Old Things, Kutztown, Pennsylvania.* $125+

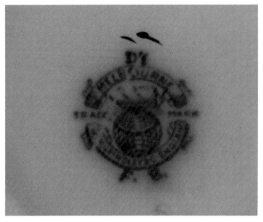

W. H. Grindley & Company Ltd., Tunstall, Staffordshire, England,
printed globe and ship mark surrounded by banners with
manufacturer's name in the lower banner and MELBORNE pattern name in the upper banner, circa 1891 - 1914. *Courtesy of Louise
and Charles Loehr, Louise's Old Things, Kutztown, Pennsylvania.*

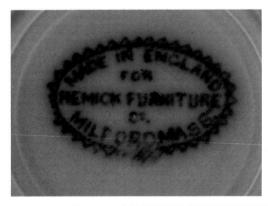

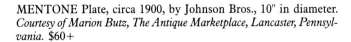

Unidentified manufacturer of MARTHA WASHINGTON pattern plate. This was produced specifically for the Remick Furniture Company of Milford, Massachusetts, 1900. This was a simple
process of changing the back mark. *Courtesy of Louise and Charles
Loehr, Louise's Old Things, Kutztown, Pennsylvania.*

MENTONE Plate, circa 1900, by Johnson Bros., 10" in diameter.
*Courtesy of Marion Butz, The Antique Marketplace, Lancaster, Pennsyl-
vania.* $60+

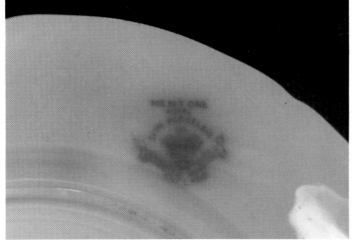

Johnson Bros. Ltd., Hanley & Tunstall, Staffordshire, England, printed crown and banner mark with manufacturer's name within the banner and MENTONE pattern name above the crown, circa 1900. *Courtesy of Marion Butz, The Antique Marketplace, Lancaster, Pennsylvania.*

MENTONE Cream Pitcher and Sugar Bowl, circa 1900, by Johnson Bros. The cream pitcher measures 4" tall and the sugar bowl measures 6" tall. *Courtesy of Marion Butz, The Antique Marketplace, Lancaster, Pennsylvania.* $225+

MENTONE Sauce Bowl, circa 1900, by Johnson Bros., 5" in diameter. *Courtesy of Marion Butz, The Antique Marketplace, Lancaster, Pennsylvania.* $25

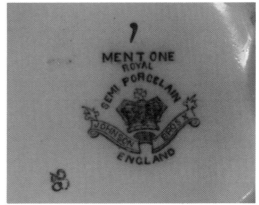

Johnson Bros. Ltd., Hanley & Tunstall, Staffordshire, England, printed crown and banner mark with manufacturer's name within the banner and MENTONE pattern name above the crown, circa 1900. *Courtesy of Marion Butz, The Antique Marketplace, Lancaster, Pennsylvania.*

Johnson Bros. Ltd., Hanley & Tunstall, Staffordshire, England, printed crown and banner mark with manufacturer's name within the banner and MENTONE pattern name above the crown, circa 1900. *Courtesy of Marion Butz, The Antique Marketplace, Lancaster, Pennsylvania.*

MENTONE Butter Dish with Insert, circa 1900, by Johnson Bros., 4" tall. *Courtesy of Marion Butz, The Antique Marketplace, Lancaster, Pennsylvania.* $125+

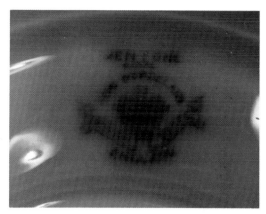

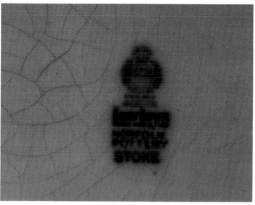

Johnson Bros. Ltd., Hanley & Tunstall, Staffordshire, England, printed crown and banner mark with manufacturer's name within the banner and MENTONE pattern name above the crown, circa 1900. *Courtesy of Marion Butz, The Antique Marketplace, Lancaster, Pennsylvania.*

Lawleys Norfolk Pottery, Stoke, Staffordshire, England, printed crown and globe mark with manufacturer's name beneath the mark, no pattern name, circa 1891 - 1902. *Courtesy of Louise and Charles Loehr, Louise's Old Things, Kutztown, Pennsylvania.*

MINTON Jardinere, circa 1891 - 1902, by Lawleys Norfolk Pottery, 8" tall x 10" in diameter. Courtesy of Louise and Charles Loehr, Louise's Old Things, Kutztown, Pennsylvania. $450+

Johnson Bros. Ltd., Hanley, Staffordshire, England, printed crown mark with manufacturer's name and MONGOLIA pattern name, circa 1900. *Courtesy of Linda Machalski, L. G. Antiques, Hartley, Delaware.*

MONGOLIA Platter, circa 1913, by Johnson Bros., 14 1/4" x 10 1/2". *Courtesy of Linda Machalski, L. G. Antiques, Hartley, Delaware.* $175+

NAPIER Covered Vegetable Dish with Underplate, circa 1900, printed crown mark without manufacturer's name. The vegetable dish measures 9" x 7" x 2 1/2". The underplate measures 11" x 8". Courtesy of John and Nancy Harner, Dover Antique Mart, Smyrna, Delaware. $150

Unidentified printed crown mark with no manufacturer's name, NAPIER pattern name, circa 1900. *Courtesy of John and Nancy Harner, Dover Antique Mart, Smyrna, Delaware.*

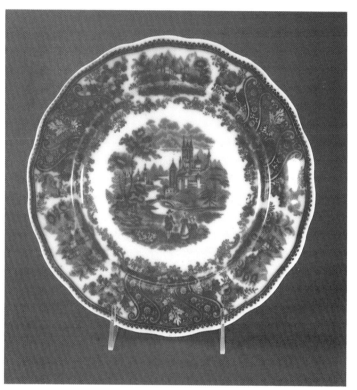

NONPARIEL Plate, circa 1891, by Burgess & Leigh, 10" in diameter. *Courtesy of John and Nancy Harner, Dover Antique Mart, Smyrna, Delaware.* $100+

Burgess & Leigh (Ltd.), Burslem, Staffordshire, England, printed mark with manufacturer's name in the center along with NONPARIEL pattern name, circa 1891 - 1919. *Courtesy of John and Nancy Harner, Dover Antique Mart, Smyrna, Delaware.*

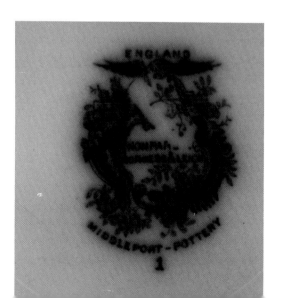

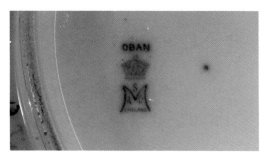

Myott, Sons & Company (Ltd.), Stoke & Cobridge, Staffordshire, England, printed crown mark with manufacturer's initials and OBAN pattern name, circa 1900. *Courtesy of Linda Machalski, L. G. Antiques, Hartley, Delaware.*

THE OLYMPIC Plate, 1915, by W. H. Grindley & Company, 8" in diameter. *Courtesy of Louise and Charles Loehr, Louise's Old Things, Kutztown, Pennsylvania.* $40

W. H. Grindley & Company Ltd., Tunstall, Staffordshire, England, printed laurel mark with manufacturer's name and THE OLYMPIC pattern name, 1915. *Courtesy of Louise and Charles Loehr, Louise's Old Things, Kutztown, Pennsylvania.*

OBAN Wash Pitcher and Basin, circa 1900, by Myott, Sons & Company. The pitcher measures 18" x 12" x 5" and the basin measures 12" in diameter. This is a rare piece, the pattern is very uncommon. *Courtesy of Linda Machalski, L. G. Antiques, Hartley, Delaware.* $700-900 set

THE OLYMPIC Vegetable Bowl, 1915, by W. H. Grindley & Company, 8" in diameter. *Courtesy of Louise and Charles Loehr, Louise's Old Things, Kutztown, Pennsylvania.* $40

OYAMA matched set of candlesticks by Doulton and Company, c. 1891, 6.5" high. *Courtesy of Arnold Kowalsky.* $550+ set.

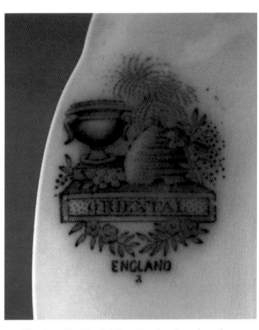

Ridgways, Hanley, Staffordshire, England, printed urn and bee-hive mark and ORIENTAL pattern name, circa 1891 - 1920. *Courtesy of Louise and Charles Loehr, Louise's Old Things, Kutztown, Pennsylvania.*

ORIENTAL Plate, circa 1891, by Ridgways, 9" in diameter. *Courtesy of Louise and Charles Loehr, Louise's Old Things, Kutztown, Pennsylvania.* $50+

OSBORNE Oval Platter, circa 1905, by Ridgways, 12 1/4" x 8 3/4". *Courtesy of Louise and Charles Loehr, Louise's Old Things, Kutztown, Pennsylvania.* $100+

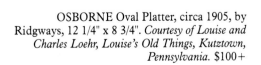

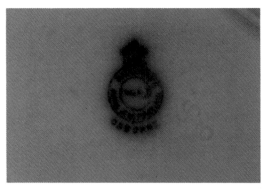

Ridgways, Hanley, Staffordshire, England, printed crown and circle mark with manufacturer's name beneath the crown and OSBORNE pattern name below the circle, circa 1905. *Courtesy of Louise and Charles Loehr, Louise's Old Things, Kutztown, Pennsylvania.*

OSBORNE Oval Vegetable Dish, circa 1905, by Ridgways, 9" x 6 3/4". *Courtesy of Louise and Charles Loehr, Louise's Old Things, Pennsylvania.* $75+

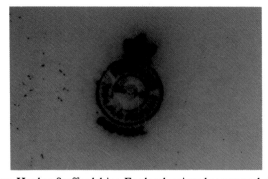

Ridgways, Hanley, Staffordshire, England, printed crown and circle mark with manufacturer's name beneath the crown and OSBORNE pattern name below the circle, circa 1905. *Courtesy of Louise and Charles Loehr, Louise's Old Things, Kutztown, Pennsylvania.*

OXFORD Plate, circa 1900 - 1912, by Johnson Bros., 9 7/8" in diameter. *Courtesy of Louise and Charles Loehr, Louise's Old Things, Kutztown, Pennsylvania.* $85-110

Johnson Bros. Ltd., Hanley, Staffordshire, England, printed crown mark with manufacturer's name and OXFORD pattern name, circa 1900 - 1912. *Courtesy of Louise and Charles Loehr, Louise's Old Things, Kutztown, Pennsylvania.*

PAISLEY Plate, circa 1901, by Mercer Pottery Company, 8" in diameter. *Courtesy of Marion Butz, The Antique Marketplace, Lancaster, Pennsylvania.* $75+

Mercer Pottery Company, Trenton, New Jersey, printed crown and shield mark with manufacturer's name across shield, no pattern name, circa 1902. *Courtesy of Marion Butz, The Antique Marketplace, Lancaster, Pennsylvania.*

Arthur J. Wilkinson (Ltd.), Burslem, Staffordshire, England, printed mark, no manufacturer's name, printed PEKIN pattern name in banner in center of mark, 1909. *Courtesy of Louise and Charles Loehr, Louise's Old Things, Kutztown, Pennsylvania.*

PAISLEY Butter Pat, 1890, by Mercer Pottery Company without printed or impressed mark, manufacturer's name or pattern name, 3 1/8" in diameter. *Courtesy of Louise and Charles Loehr, Louise's Old Things, Kutztown, Pennsylvania.* $30-40

PERSIAN MOSS Plate, 1891, unidentified German crown and shield mark (possibly Utzchneider & Company), 7 7/8" in diameter. *Courtesy of Louise and Charles Loehr, Louise's Old Things, Kutztown, Pennsylvania.* $40+

PEKIN Platter, 1909, by Arthur J. Wilkinson (Ltd.), 18 1/2" x 13 7/8". *Courtesy of Louise and Charles Loehr, Louise's Old Things, Kutztown, Pennsylvania.* $250+

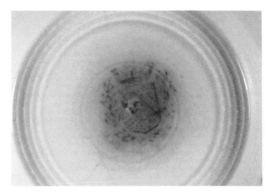

Unidentified printed German crown and shield mark (possibly Utzchneider & Company), no printed or impressed pattern name, circa 1891. *Courtesy of John and Nancy Harner, Dover Antique Mart, Smyrna, Delaware.*

PERSIAN MOSS Round Vegetable Bowl, 1891, unidentified German crown and shield mark (possibly Utzchneider & Company), 8 1/4" in diameter. *Courtesy of Louise and Charles Loehr, Louise's Old Things, Kutztown, Pennsylvania.* $85+

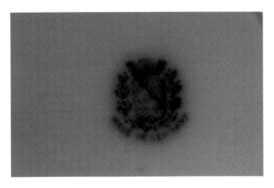

Unidentified printed German crown and shield mark (possibly Utzchneider & Company), no printed or impressed pattern name, circa 1891. *Courtesy of Louise and Charles Loehr, Louise's Old Things, Kutztown, Pennsylvania.*

PERSIAN MOSS Bowl, 1891, unidentified German crown and shield mark (possibly Utzchneider & Company), 3" tall x 5 1/4" in diameter. *Courtesy of John and Nancy Harner, Dover Antique Mart, Smyrna, Delaware.* $50+

PERSIAN SPRAY Plate, 1882 - 1902, by Doulton and Company, 9 1/4" in diameter. Courtesy of Louise and Charles Loehr, Louise's Old Things, Kutztown, Pennsylvania. $60+

Doulton and Company (Ltd.), Burslem, Staffordshire, England, printed and impressed crown and circle mark with manufacturer's name, no pattern name, circa 1882 - 1902. "England" added to the mark in 1891. *Courtesy of Louise and Charles Loehr, Louise's Old Things, Kutztown, Pennsylvania.*

PERSIAN SPRAY 1 1/2 qt. Covered Vegetable Bowl, 1882 - 1902, by Doulton and Company, 7 1/2" x 7 1/4". *Courtesy of Louise and Charles Loehr, Louise's Old Things, Kutztown, Pennsylvania.* $125+

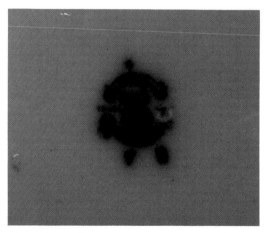

PERTH Chamber Pot, 1891 - 1914, by W. H. Grindley and Company, 5" tall x 9" in diameter. *Courtesy of Louise and Charles Loehr, Louise's Old Things, Kutztown, Pennsylvania.* $125+

W. H. Grindley & Company Ltd., Tunstall, Staffordshire, England, printed globe and ship mark surrounded by banners with manufacturer's name in the lower banner and PERTH pattern name in the upper banner, circa 1891 - 1914. *Courtesy of Louise and Charles Loehr, Louise's Old Things, Kutztown, Pennsylvania.*

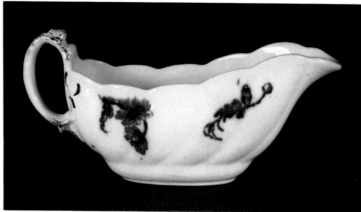

POPPY Gravy Boat, circa 1891 - 1914, by W. H. Grindley and Company, 9" x 3" x 4". *Courtesy of John and Nancy Harner, Dover Antique Mart, Smyrna, Delaware.* $85-110

PICKWICK Plate (souvenir ware), 1903, by Ridgways, 10" in diameter. A lively series of plates portrays Charles Dicken's Mr. Pickwick character. This one is titled "Mr. Pickwick and the Rival Editors." *Courtesy of Louise and Charles Loehr, Louise's Old Things, Kutztown, Pennsylvania.* $125+

W. H. Grindley & Company Ltd., Tunstall, Staffordshire, England, printed globe and ship mark surrounded by banners with manufacturer's name in the lower banner and POPPY pattern name in the upper banner, circa 1891 - 1914. *Courtesy of John and Nancy Harner, Dover Antique Mart, Smyrna, Delaware.*

THE PORTRAICTUER OF CAPTAYNE JOHN SMITH ADMIRALL OF NEW ENGLAND Plate (souvenir ware), c. 1906, by Rowland & Marsellus Co., 10" diameter. *Courtesy of John and Nancy Harner, Dover Antique Mart, Smyrna, Delaware.* $125+

Ridgways, Hanley, Staffordshire, England, printed mark with manufacturer's name and PICKWICK pattern name. The registration number indicates a 1903 registry date. *Courtesy of Louise and Charles Loehr, Louise's Old Things, Kutztown, Pennsylvania.*

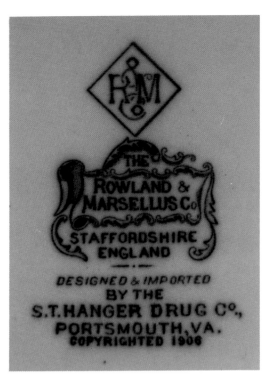

Johnson Bros. Ltd., Hanley, Staffordshire, England, printed crown mark with manufacturer's name and PRINCETON pattern name, circa 1900 - 1912. *Courtesy of John and Nancy Harner, Dover Antique Mart, Smyrna, Delaware.*

Rowland & Marsellus Company, Longton, Staffordshire, England, printed diamond mark with manufacturer's initials, no pattern name, 1860 - 1906+. *Courtesy of John and Nancy Harner, Dover Antique Mart, Smyrna, Delaware.*

THE REGAL Compote, circa 1900, by W. H. Grindley and Company. The compote measures 4 3/4" tall and the plate top measures 10" in diameter. *Courtesy of Louise and Charles Loehr, Louise's Old Things, Kutztown, Pennsylvania.* $275-350

PRINCETON Platter, circa 1900 - 1912, by Johnson Bros., 12 3/4" x 9 1/2". *Courtesy of John and Nancy Harner, Dover Antique Mart, Smyrna, Delaware.* $125+

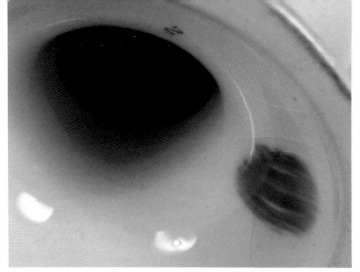

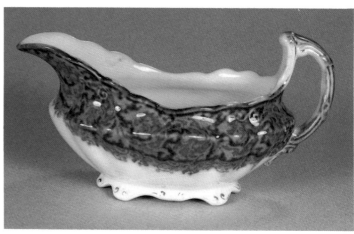

W. H. Grindley & Company Ltd., Tunstall, Staffordshire, England, printed globe and ship mark surrounded by banners with manufacturer's name in the lower banner and THE REGAL pattern name in the upper banner, circa 1891 - 1914. Become familiar with the basic shapes of the most common marks. The "clarity" of this mark is very common among Flow Blue. When the pattern flows, so does the mark. *Courtesy of Louise and Charles Loehr, Louise's Old Things, Kutztown, Pennsylvania.*

RIALTO Gravy Boat, circa 1896, by John Maddock & Sons, 3" tall x 6 1/2". *Courtesy of Louise and Charles Loehr, Louise's Old Things, Kutztown, Pennsylvania.* $85-110

John Maddock & Sons, Ltd., Burslem, Staffordshire, England, printed crown and circle mark with manufacturer's name below the crown and RIALTO pattern name beneath the mark, circa 1896. *Courtesy of Louise and Charles Loehr, Louise's Old Things, Kutztown, Pennsylvania.*

REGINA Soup Bowl, 1887, by Sociêtê Cêramique, 7 1/2" in diameter. *Courtesy of Louise and Charles Loehr, Louise's Old Things, Kutztown, Pennsylvania.* $50+

Sociêtê Cêramique, Maastricht, Holland, printed mark with manufacturer's name and REGINA pattern name, 1887. *Courtesy of Louise and Charles Loehr, Louise's Old Things, Kutztown, Pennsylvania.*

RICHMOND Soup Bowl, circa 1912, by Johnson Bros., 8" in diameter. *Courtesy of Marion Butz, The Antique Marketplace, Lancaster, Pennsylvania.* $50

Johnson Bros. Ltd., Hanley, Staffordshire, England, printed crown mark with manufacturer's name and RICHMOND pattern name, circa 1900 - 1912. *Courtesy of Marion Butz, The Antique Marketplace, Lancaster, Pennsylvania.*

W. H. Grindley & Company Ltd., Tunstall, Staffordshire, England, printed globe and ship mark surrounded by banners with manufacturer's name in the lower banner and ROSE pattern name in the upper banner, c. 1891 - 1914. The registration number (Rd. No.) indicates the year of registration was 1893. *Courtesy of John and Nancy Harner, Dover Antique Mart, Smyrna, Delaware.*

ROSE Covered Vegetable Bowl, circa 1893, by W. H. Grindley, 11" x 7" x 5". *Courtesy of John and Nancy Harner, Dover Antique Mart, Smyrna, Delaware.* $200+

SAVOY Plate, circa 1900 - 1912, by Johnson Bros., 9" in diameter. *Courtesy of Linda Machalski, L. G. Antiques, Hartley, Delaware.* $65+

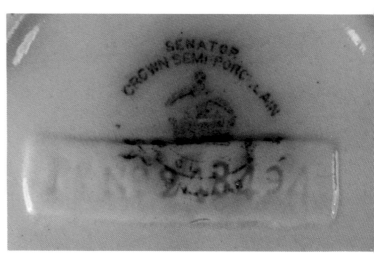

Johnson Bros. Ltd., Hanley, Staffordshire, England, printed crown mark with manufacturer's name and SAVOY pattern name, circa 1900 - 1912. *Courtesy of Linda Machalski, L. G. Antiques, Hartley, Delaware.*

SENATOR Sugar Bowl, circa 1895, by J. Dimmock & Company, 6 1/2" tall. Courtesy of Louise and Charles Loehr, Louise's Old Things, Kutztown, Pennsylvania. $125-150

SAVOY Platter, circa 1900 - 1912, by Johnson Bros., 12 1/2" x 9 1/2". *Courtesy of Louise and Charles Loehr, Louise's Old Things, Pennsylvania.* $110+

Johnson Bros. Ltd., Hanley, Staffordshire, England, printed crown mark with manufacturer's name and SAVOY pattern name, circa 1900 - 1912. *Courtesy of Louise and Charles Loehr, Louise's Old Things, Kutztown, Pennsylvania.*

J. Dimmock & Company, Hanley, Staffordshire, England, printed crown and banner mark with proprietor's name CLIFF (W. D. Cliff since circa 1878) in the banner beneath the crown and SENATOR pattern name above the mark, circa 1878 - 1904. The impressed registration number (Rd. No.) indicates the year of registration was 1895. *Courtesy of Louise and Charles Loehr, Louise's Old Things, Kutztown, Pennsylvania.*

SHANGHI Platter, circa 1891, by W. H. Grindley & Company, 15 1/4" x 11". *Courtesy of Bonne Hohl.* $150+

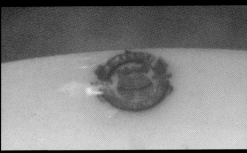

W. H. Grindley & Company Ltd., Tunstall, Staffordshire, England, printed globe and ship mark surrounded by banners with manufacturer's name in the lower banner and SHANGHI pattern name in the upper banner, circa 1891 - 1914. *Courtesy of Bonne Hohl.*

SHANGHI Bouillon Cup & Saucer, circa 1914, by W. H. Grindley & Company. The bouillon cup measures 2 1/2" tall x 3 3/4" in diameter. The saucer measures 5 7/8" in diameter. *Courtesy of Bonne Hohl.* $125+

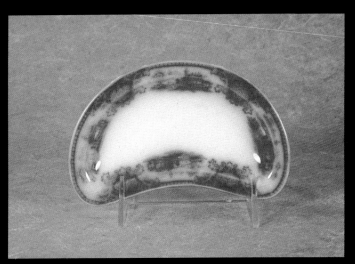

SHANGHI Bone Dish, circa 1891, by W. H. Grindley & Company, 6 1/4" in length. Courtesy of Bonne Hohl. $75+

W. H. Grindley & Company Ltd., Tunstall, Staffordshire, England, printed laurel mark with manufacturer's name in the center and no pattern name, circa 1914 - 1925. *Courtesy of Bonne Hohl.*

SHANGHI Teapot, circa 1891, by W. H. Grindley & Company, 5 3/8" tall. *Courtesy of Bonne Hohl.* $600+

SPODE "LANDSCAPE" Sauce Tureen with Underplate and Ladle, 1891, by W. T. Copeland. The tureen measures 5 1/2" tall and the underplate measures 8 7/8" x 6 7/8". The ladle measures 7" in length. *Courtesy of Louise and Charles Loehr, Louise's Old Things, Kutztown, Pennsylvania.* $375+

SPODE "LANDSCAPE" Platter, 1891, by W. T. Copeland, 17" x 12 5/8". *Courtesy of Louise and Charles Loehr, Louise's Old Things, Kutztown, Pennsylvania.* $200+

W. T. Copeland (& Sons Ltd.), Stoke, Staffordshire, England, printed manufacturer's name and SPODE "LANDSCAPE", circa 1891. *Courtesy of Louise and Charles Loehr, Louise's Old Things, Kutztown, Pennsylvania.*

W. T. Copeland (& Sons Ltd.), Stoke, Staffordshire, England, printed and impressed manufacturer's name and SPODE "LANDSCAPE", circa 1891. *Courtesy of Louise and Charles Loehr, Louise's Old Things, Kutztown, Pennsylvania.*

SPODE'S TOWER Plate, 1891, by W. T. Copeland, 9 1/4" in diameter. *Courtesy of Linda Machalski, L. G. Antiques, Hartley, Delaware.* $45+

W. T. Copeland (& Sons Ltd.), Stoke, Staffordshire, England, printed manufacturer's name and SPODE' S TOWER, circa 1891. *Courtesy of Linda Machalski, L. G. Antiques, Hartley, Delaware.*

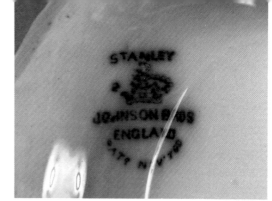

Johnson Bros. Ltd., Hanley, Staffordshire, England, printed crown mark with manufacturer's name and STANLEY pattern name, circa 1900 - 1912. *Courtesy of Louise and Charles Loehr, Louise's Old Things, Kutztown, Pennsylvania.*

TOURAINE Plate, circa 1898, by Henry Alcock & Company, 8 1/2" in diameter. *Courtesy of Marion Butz, The Antique Marketplace, Lancaster, Pennsylvania.* $65+

Henry Alcock & Company, Cobridge, Staffordshire, England, printed crown and shield mark with manufacturer's name, no pattern name, 1880 - 1910. The registration number places the date of registry as 1898. *Courtesy of Marion Butz, The Antique Marketplace, Lancaster, Pennsylvania.*

STANLEY Individual Vegetable Bowl, 1900, by Johnson Bros., 5 1/2" x 4 3/8". *Courtesy of Louise and Charles Loehr, Louise's Old Things, Kutztown, Pennsylvania.* $85-110

TOURAINE Butter Pat, circa 1880 - 1910, no printed or impressed mark or pattern name, 3" in diameter. *Courtesy of Jacqueline Hunsicker.* $50-65

Henry Alcock & Company, Cobridge, Staffordshire, England, printed crown and shield mark with manufacturer's name and TOURAINE pattern name, 1891 - 1910. *Courtesy of Jacqueline Hunsicker.*

TOURAINE Gravy Boat and Underplate, circa 1891 - 1931. The gravy boat was produced by Stanley Pottery Company and the underplate was potted by Henry Alcock & Company Ltd. The gravy boat measures 3" tall x 6 1/2" in width and the underplate measures 8" x 5 1/2". *Courtesy of Jacqueline Hunsicker.* $275+

Stanley Pottery Company, Longton, Staffordshire, England, printed crown mark with manufacturer's name and TOURAINE pattern name. The dating of this mark is ambiguous as Stanley marks were printed by Colclough & Company using the Stanley name from 1903 - 1919 and by Stanley Pottery from 1928 - 1931. The registry mark indicates a registration date of 1898. *Courtesy of Jacqueline Hunsicker.*

TOURAINE Covered Butter Dish, circa 1903 - 1931, by Stanley Pottery Company, 4 1/2" tall x 7 1/4" in diameter. *Courtesy of Jacqueline Hunsicker.* $375+

Stanley Pottery Company, Longton, Staffordshire, England, printed crown mark with manufacturer's name and TOURAINE pattern name. The dating of this mark is ambiguous as Stanley marks were printed by Colclough & Company using the Stanley name from 1903 - 1919 and by Stanley Pottery from 1928 - 1931. The registry mark indicates a registration date of 1898. Collectors need to be aware that the Touraine pattern is currently being reproduced. *Courtesy of Jacqueline Hunsicker.*

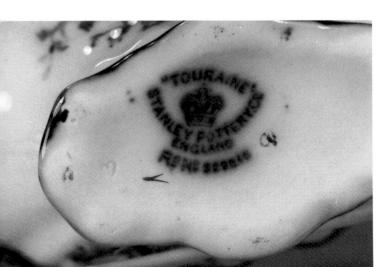

Wood & Son(s Ltd.), Burslem, Staffordshire, England, printed crown and banner mark with manufacturer's name in the banner beneath the crown and TRILBY pattern name in the banner above, 1891 - 1907. *Courtesy of Louise and Charles Loehr, Louise's Old Things, Kutztown, Pennsylvania.*

TOURAINE Egg Cup, circa 1891 - 1931; no printed or impressed mark or pattern name, 3 1/4" tall x 2 1/4" in diameter. *Courtesy of Jacqueline Hunsicker.* $250+

TRILBY Vegetable Bowl, circa 1891, by Wood & Son, 9 1/2" in diameter. *Courtesy of Jacqueline Hunsicker.* $50+

TRILBY Cake Plate, circa 1891, by Wood & Son, 10 1/4" in diameter. Printed advertisment "Compliments John A. Hedin & Co. Furniture & Carpet" across face of plate. *Courtesy of Louise and Charles Loehr, Louise's Old Things, Kutztown, Pennsylvania.* $75+

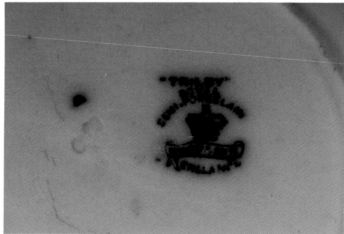

Wood & Son(s Ltd.), Burslem, Staffordshire, England, printed crown and banner mark with manufacturer's name in the banner beneath the crown and TRILBY pattern name in the banner above, 1891 - 1907. *Courtesy of Jacqueline Hunsicker.*

Unidentified Pedistaled Cake Stand, circa 1902, by Mercer Pottery Company, The cake stand measures 4 3/4" tall and the plate top measures 10" in diameter. *Courtesy of John and Nancy Harner, Dover Antique Mart, Smyrna, Delaware.* $110+

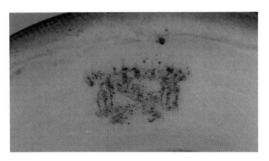

Mercer Pottery Company, Trenton, New Jersey, printed crown and shield mark with manufacturer's name across shield, no pattern name, circa 1902. Once again, it pays to become familiar with the general shape of marks as the details often become lost in the firing of the glaze. *Courtesy of John and Nancy Harner, Dover Antique Mart, Smyrna, Delaware.*

Unidentified Floral Pattern Bowl, 1893 - 1898, by Warwick China Company, 6" in diameter. *Courtesy of John and Nancy Harner, Dover Antique Mart, Smyrna, Delaware.* $30-50

Warwick China Company, Wheeling, West Virginia, printed manufacturer's name, no pattern name, 1893 - 1898. *Courtesy of John and Nancy Harner, Dover Antique Mart, Smyrna, Delaware.*

These are not Flow Blue. Be aware, some items which may appear to be Flow Blue at first glance are not, including these unidentified scenic trivets, c. 1903, by Royal Copenhagen Porcelain Factory, 3 1/4" dia. *Courtesy of Linda Machalski, L. G. Antiques, Hartley, Delaware.*

Royal Copenhagen Porcelain Factory Ltd., Fredericksberg, Denmark, printed mark, no pattern name, 1903 - present. *Courtesy of Linda Machalski, L. G. Antiques, Hartley, Delaware.*

These also are not Flow Blue. Two more examples of this type, scenic trivets, c, 1903, by Royal Copenhagen Porcelain Factory. *Courtesy of Linda Machalski, L. G. Antiques, Hartley, Delaware.*

Unidentified Sprig Pattern Platter, circa 1900, no mark, no pattern name, 18 1/2" x 15". *Courtesy of Louise and Charles Loehr, Louise's Old Things, Kutztown, Pennsylvania.* $175-225

Royal Copenhagen Porcelain Factory Ltd., Copenhagen, Denmark, printed crown and circle mark with manufacturer's name, no pattern name, 1922 - present. *Courtesy of Linda Machalski, L. G. Antiques, Hartley, Delaware.*

Unidentified Butter Pat, circa 1900, no mark, no pattern name, 3 1/8" in diameter. *Courtesy of Marion Butz, The Antique Marketplace, Lancaster, Pennsylvania.* $30-40

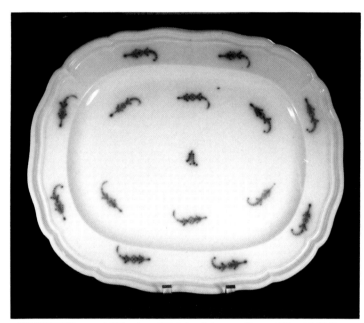

VENICE Platter, 1895, circa 1900, by Johnson Bros., 18" x 13 3/4". *Courtesy of Louise and Charles Loehr, Louise's Old Things, Kutztown, Pennsylvania.* $175-225

Johnson Bros. Ltd., Hanley & Tunstall, Staffordshire, England, printed crown and banner mark with manufacturer's name within the banner and VENICE pattern name above the crown, circa 1900. The registry mark indicates an 1895 date of registry. *Courtesy of Louise and Charles Loehr, Louise's Old Things, Kutztown, Pennsylvania.*

VERMONT Dinner Set, 1906 - 1912, by Burgess & Leigh. Dinner anyone? This is a nearly complete set illustrating just how impressive a table set in Flow Blue could look. *Courtesy of Linda Machalski, L. G. Antiques, Hartley, Delaware.* $2500+

VERMONT Luncheon Set, 1906 - 1912, by Burgess & Leigh. From left to right and back to front: luncheon plate, 8" in diameter; sugar bowl, 6 1/4" tall; teapot, 7 1/2" tall; tea cup, 2 1/2" tall x 3 1/4" in diameter; saucer, 6" in diameter; cream pitcher, 6" tall. Courtesy of Linda Machalski, L. G. Antiques, Hartley, Delaware. $600-750

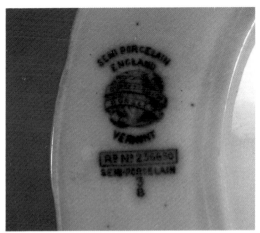

Burgess & Leigh (Ltd.), Burslem, Staffordshire, England, printed globe and banner mark with manufacturer's name in banner and VERMONT pattern name beneath the globe, 1906 - 1912. The registration number indicates an 1894 date of registry. *Courtesy of Linda Machalski, L. G. Antiques, Hartley, Delaware.*

VERMONT Bowl, 1906 - 1912, by Burgess & Leigh, 9" in diameter. *Courtesy of John and Nancy Harner, Dover Antique Mart, Smyrna, Delaware.* $40-60

VERMONT Plate, 1906 - 1912, by Burgess & Leigh, 9" in diameter. *Courtesy of Linda Machalski, L. G. Antiques, Hartley, Delaware.* $40-60

Burgess & Leigh (Ltd.), Burslem, Staffordshire, England, printed globe and banner mark with manufacturer's name in banner and VERMONT pattern name beneath the globe, 1906 - 1912. The registration number indicates an 1894 date of registry. *Courtesy of John and Nancy Harner, Dover Antique Mart, Smyrna, Delaware.*

VERMONT Platter and Vegetable Dish, 1906 - 1912, by Burgess and Leigh. The platter measures 10" x 7" and the vegetable dish measures 10" x 7" x 5". *Courtesy of Linda Machalski, L. G. Antiques, Hartley, Delaware.* Platter: $125+; dish: $200+

VERMONT Butter Dish, 1906 - 1912, by Burgess and Leigh, 8" x 7" x 4". *Courtesy of Linda Machalski, L. G. Antiques, Hartley, Delaware.* $250+

VERMONT Waste Bowl, 1906 - 1912, by Burgess and Leigh, 3" tall x 5" in diameter. *Courtesy of Linda Machalski, L. G. Antiques, Hartley, Delaware.* $125+

Wood & Son(s Ltd.), Burslem, Staffordshire, England, printed crown and banner mark with manufacturer's name within the banner below the crown and the VICTORIA pattern name within the upper banner, 1891 - 1907. *Courtesy of John and Nancy Harner, Dover Antique Mart, Smyrna, Delaware.*

VERONA Oval Platter, 1897, by Alfred Meakin, 12 1/4". *Courtesy of Louise and Charles Loehr, Louise's Old Things, Kutztown, Pennsylvania.* $100+

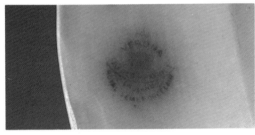

Alfred Meakin (Ltd.), Tunstall, Staffordshire, England, printed crown and banner mark with manufacturer's name in the banner and VERONA pattern name above the crown, circa 1891 - 1930. *Courtesy of Louise and Charles Loehr, Louise's Old Things, Kutztown, Pennsylvania.*

WALDORF Plate, circa 1890 - 1894, by New Wharf Pottery Company, 9" in diameter. This is a very similar pattern to LUZERNE by Mercer Pottery Company. Collectors should be aware that the Waldorf pattern is currently being reproduced. *Courtesy of Linda Machalski, L. G. Antiques, Hartley, Delaware.* $75-95

VICTORIA Bowl, 1891 - 1907, by Wood & Son, 10 1/4" in diameter. *Courtesy of John and Nancy Harner, Dover Antique Mart, Smyrna, Delaware.* $75+

New Wharf Pottery Company, Burslem, Staffordshire, England, printed Staffordshire knot and crown mark with manufacturer's name below the knot and WALDORF pattern name in a banner above the crown, circa 1890 - 1894. *Courtesy of Linda Machalski, L. G. Antiques, Hartley, Delaware.*

WATTEAU Berry/Dessert Bowl, circa 1909, no manufacturer's name, 5" in diameter. *Courtesy of Louise and Charles Loehr, Louise's Old Things, Kutztown, Pennsylvania.* $20-40

Unidentified manufacturer with printed crown and circle mark and WATTEAU pattern name beneath the crown, circa 1909. *Courtesy of Louise and Charles Loehr, Louise's Old Things, Kutztown, Pennsylvania.*

WATTEAU Covered Vegetable Tureen, circa 1930, by Doulton & Company, 7" tall x 11" in length. *Courtesy of Louise and Charles Loehr, Louise's Old Things, Kutztown, Pennsylvania.* $250-350

Doulton & Company (Ltd.), Burslem, Staffordshire, England, printed urn and banner mark with manufacturer's name beneath the banner and WATTEAU pattern name within the banner, circa 1930. *Courtesy of Louise and Charles Loehr, Louise's Old Things, Kutztown, Pennsylvania.*

WILLOW Plate, circa 1882 - 1890, Doulton & Company, 9 3/8" in diameter. *Courtesy of Louise and Charles Loehr, Louise's Old Things, Kutztown, Pennsylvania.* $50-60

Doulton & Company (Ltd.), Burslem, Staffordshire, England, printed manufacturer's name and WILLOW pattern name, circa 1882 - 1890. *Courtesy of Louise and Charles Loehr, Louise's Old Things, Kutztown, Pennsylvania.*

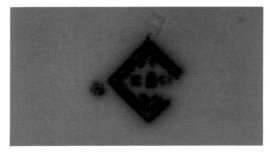

Keeling & Company, Burslem, Staffordshire, England, printed diamond shaped mark with manufacturer's initials (K & Co.) in the center, no pattern name, 1886 - 1891. *Courtesy of Louise and Charles Loehr, Louise's Old Things, Kutztown, Pennsylvania.*

WILLOW Pedestaled Bowl, 1891, by Doulton & Company, 6 1/4" tall x 9 1/4" in diameter. This is an excellent example of the attributes which made Flow Blue popular, a deep blue color and a romantic, sentimental design. *Courtesy of Louise and Charles Loehr, Louise's Old Things, Kutztown, Pennsylvania.* $700+

Doulton & Company (Ltd.), Burslem, Staffordshire, England, printed crown and circle mark with manufacturer's name within the circle and WILLOW pattern name beneath the mark, circa 1891 - 1902. *Courtesy of Louise and Charles Loehr, Louise's Old Things, Kutztown, Pennsylvania.*

WILLOW Plate, 1886, by Keeling & Company, 7 3/4" in diameter. A very different pattern from Doulton's WILLOW. *Courtesy of Louise and Charles Loehr, Louise's Old Things, Kutztown, Pennsylvania.* $30-50

Chapter 6
Miscellany

Combed Ware

Not to be confused with 18th century combed lead glazed slipware dishes which are a different animal entirely. Our combed ware is defined as pottery decorated with a marbled effect, produced by combing while the glaze is wet. Combing is a process of drawing a comb or wire brush across wet, freshly applied color or colors on the surface of pottery to create a zigzag or waving pattern.[1]

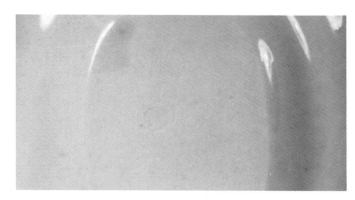

Thomas Dimmock & Company, Shelton, Staffordshire, England, impressed "D" manufacturer's initial, no impressed or printed pattern name, 1828 - 1859. *Courtesy of Louise and Charles Loehr, Louise's Old Things, Kutztown, Pennsylvania.*

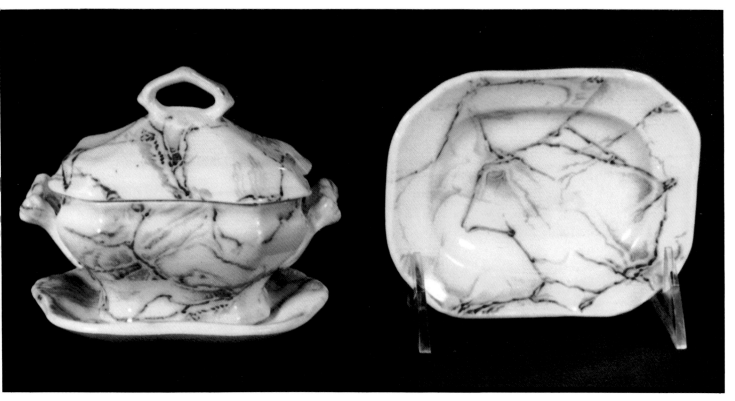

"MARBLE" Child's Soup Tureen with Underplate and Platter, 1840, by Thomas Dimmock. The soup tureen measures 4 1/2" x 3 1/2" x 4", the underplate meaures 4 1/4" x 3" and the platter measures 4 1/2" x 3 1/2". This is part of a complete child's dinner service. *Courtesy of Louise and Charles Loehr, Louise's Old Things, Kutztown, Pennsylvania.* $350+ set

Ground Patterns

Diapered or figured patterns filling in borders and undecorated backgrounds. "Cracked Ice" has broken straight
lines forming irregular squares, mimicking the markings of
cracked ice. It is painted in dark blue on a lighter blue ground.[2]

International Pottery Company, Trenton, New Jersey, printed mark
with manufacturer's initials (I P Co.) in the center, no printed or
impressed pattern name, 1860 - 1940. *Courtesy of Louise and Charles
Loehr, Louise's Old Things, Kutztown, Pennsylvania.*

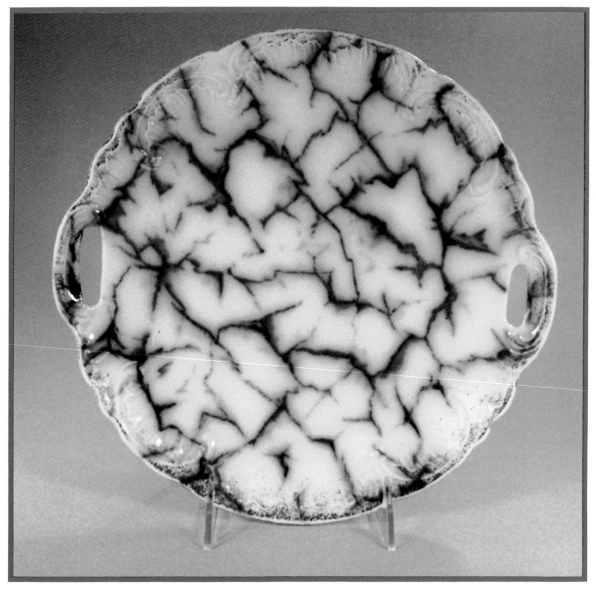

"CRACKED ICE" Cake Plate, no date, by International Pottery Company, 10 1/4" in diameter. *Courtesy of Louise and
Charles Loehr, Louise's Old Things, Kutztown, Pennsylvania.* $125+

Handpainted Wares (Arranged by pattern name):

BRUSHSTROKE Cuspidor, no date, no mark, 3 1/4" tall x 7 1/2" in diameter. *Courtesy of Louise and Charles Loehr, Louise's Old Things, Kutztown, Pennsylvania.* $400-500

BRUSHSTROKE Plate with 12 panel rim, no date, no mark, 8" in diameter. *Courtesy of Linda Machalski, L. G. Antiques, Hartley, Delaware.* $65-85

BRUSHSTROKE Octagonal Wash Pitcher and Basin, circa 1850, no mark. The pitcher measures 11 1/2" tall. The basin measures 14" in diameter. *Courtesy of Louise and Charles Loehr, Louise's Old Things, Kutztown, Pennsylvania.* $1400-1600

BRUSHSTROKE Plate, no date, no mark, 9" in diameter. *Courtesy of Linda Machalski, L. G. Antiques, Hartley, Delaware.* $40-60

"SIMPLICITAS" Toilet, circa 1900, by Doulton & Company, 16"
tall. Here is a large piece in Flow Blue you will not find every day.
This is a fully functional toilet basin designed for an overhead
water tank. *Courtesy of Bonne Hohl.* $1500+

Doulton & Company, Lambeth, London, England, printed oval
mark with manufacturer's name and SIMPLICITAS name, the dating of this peculiar mark is unclear. Doulton & Company was in
business from circa 1858 - 1956. *Courtesy of Bonne Hohl.*

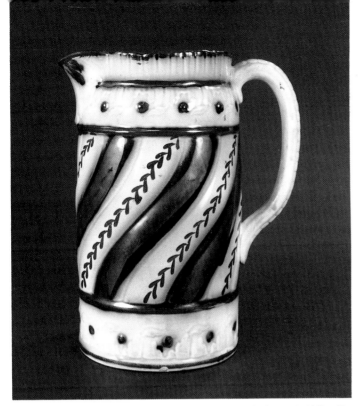

WHEEL Pitcher, 1891, by Charles Allerton & Sons, 8 1/4" tall. Copper luster highlights the hand painted design. *Courtesy of Louise and Charles Loehr, Louise's Old Things, Kutztown, Pennsylvania.* $125+

WHEEL Child's Wash Pitcher and Basin, no date, no maker's mark. The pitcher measures 6" tall and the basin measures 3" tall x 5 1/2" in diameter. Copper luster highlights the hand painted design. *Courtesy of Louise and Charles Loehr, Louise's Old Things, Kutztown, Pennsylvania.* $150+

Charles Allerton & Sons, Longton, Staffordshire, England, printed crown mark with manufacturer's name, no printed or incised pattern name, circa 1891 - 1912. *Courtesy of Louise and Charles Loehr, Louise's Old Things, Kutztown, Pennsylvania.*

WHEEL Child's Tea Service, circa 1890, no mark. Left to right: cream pitcher, 3 1/4" tall x 2 3/8" in diameter; teapot, 5" tall x 3 1/4" in diameter; sugar bowl, 4 1/2" tall x 2 3/4" in diameter; tea cup, 2 1/4" tall x 2 1/2" in diameter; saucer, 4 1/2" in diameter. Part of a complete child's set. Copper luster highlights the hand painted design. *Courtesy of Louise and Charles Loehr, Louise's Old Things, Kutztown, Pennsylvania.* $350+ set

Unidentified Patterns
Unidentified Patterns Without Marks or Date Ranges

Unidentified Floral Plate, no date, no mark, 10 1/2" in diameter. *Courtesy of Louise and Charles Loehr, Louise's Old Things, Kutztown, Pennsylvania.* $75+

Unidentified Oriental Pattern Waste Bowl Muffler, no date, no mark, 11" in diameter. *Courtesy of Louise and Charles Loehr, Louise's Old Things, Kutztown, Pennsylvania.* $125+

Flow Blue of the Modern Era: Circa 1935 to Present Day

BENTON Platter, 1946, by Longton Pottery Company Ltd., 16 3/4" x 12". *Courtesy of John and Nancy Harner, Dover Antique Mart, Smyrna, Delaware.* $75+

Longton Pottery Company Ltd., Longton, Staffordshire, England, printed banner mark with manufacturer's name below and BENTON pattern name within the banner, 1946 - 1955. *Courtesy of John and Nancy Harner, Dover Antique Mart, Smyrna, Delaware.*

Unidentified Plate, circa 1935, by Allertons, 9" in diameter. *Courtesy of Linda Machalski, L. G. Antiques, Hartley, Delaware.* $30-50

Allertons Ltd., Longton, Staffordshire, England, printed laurel mark with manufacturer's initial (A) in the center of the mark, manufacturer's name beneath the laurel and pattern name (illegible) beneath the mark, circa 1929 - 1942. *Courtesy of Linda Machalski, L. G. Antiques, Hartley, Delaware.*

VINRANKA Teapot, circa 1968, by Gefle Porcelainworks, 5" tall. *Courtesy of Marion Butz, The Antique Marketplace, Lancaster, Pennsylvania.* $250-350

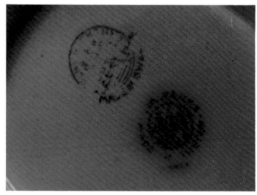

Gefle Porcelainworks, Gavle, Sweden, printed circle mark with manufacturer's name within the mark and VINRANKA pattern name above the mark, circa 1968 - present. *Courtesy of Marion Butz, The Antique Marketplace, Lancaster, Pennsylvania.*

Footnotes
[1] Edwin Atlee Barber, The Ceramic Collector's Glossary, (New York: Da Capo Press, 1967), 26.
[2] ibid, 51-52

Bibliography

Barber, Edwin Atlee. *The Ceramic Collector's Glossary.* New York: Da Capo Press, 1967.

Copeland, Robert. "A Brief History of Transfer-Printing on Blue and White Ceramics." In Kowalsky, Arnold A. and Dorothy E. *Encyclopedia of Marks On American, English and European Earthenware, Ironstone, and Stoneware 1780-1980.* Atglen, Pennsylvania: Schiffer Publishing Ltd., 1999.

Deetz, James. *In Small Things Forgotten.* Garden City, New York: Anchor Press/Doubleday, 1977.

Ewins, Neil. *Supplying the Present Wants of Our Yankee Cousins ... : Staffordshire Ceramics and the American Market 1775-1880.* Journal of Ceramic History 15, 1997.

Gaston, Mary Frank. *The Collector's Encyclopedia of Flow Blue China.* Paducah, Kentucky: Collector Books, 1983.

_____. *The Collector's Encyclopedia of Flow Blue. Second Series.* Paducah, Kentucky: Collector Books, 1994.

Godden, Geoffrey A. *British Porcelain. An Illustrated Guide.* New York: Clarkson N. Potter, Inc./Publisher, 1974.

_____. *Encyclopaedia of British Pottery and Porcelain Marks.* New York: Bonanza Books, 1964.

Hume, Ivor Noël. *All the Best Rubbish.* New York: Harper & Row, Publishers, 1974.

_____. *A Guide to Artifacts of Colonial America.* New York: Alfred A. Knopf, 1969.

_____. *If These Pots Could Talk. Collecting 2,000 Years of British Household Pottery.* Milwaukee, Wisconsin: Chipstone Foundation, 2001.

Klein, Terry H. "Nineteenth-Century Ceramics and Models of Consumer Behavior." *Historical Archaeology* 25(2), 1991, pp. 77-88.

Kovel, Ralph and Terry. *Kovels' New Dictionary of Marks.* New York: Crown Publishers, Inc., 1986.

Kowalsky, Arnold A. and Dorothy E. *Encyclopedia of Marks On American, English and European Earthenware, Iron-stone, and Stoneware 1780-1980.* Atglen, Pennsylvania: Schiffer Publishing Ltd., 1999.

Larkin, Jack. *The Reshaping of Everyday Life, 1790-1840.* New York: Harper and Row, Publishers, 1988.

MacKendrick, Russ. "Flow Blue China." *Treasure Chest* 4:8, December 1991.

Miller, George L. "Classification and Economic Scaling of Nineteenth Century Ceramics." *Historical Archaeology* 14:1, 1980.

_____. "A Revised Set of CC Index Values for Classification and Economic Scaling of English Ceramics from 1787 to 1880." *Historical Archaeology* 25:1, 1991.

Moore, N. Hudson. *The Old China Book.* New York: Tudor Publishing Company, 1903

Roberts, Gaye Blake. *True Blue.* East Hagbourne, Oxfordshire: Friends of Blue, 1998.

Snyder, Jeffrey B. *Fascinating Flow Blue.* Atglen, Pennsylvania: Schiffer Publishing Ltd., 1997.

_____. *Flow Blue. A Closer Look.* Atglen, Pennsylvania: Schiffer Publishing Ltd., 2000.

_____. *Historic Flow Blue.* Atglen, Pennsylvania: Schiffer Publishing Ltd., 1994.

_____. *A Pocket Guide to Flow Blue.* Atglen, Pennsylvania: Schiffer Publishing Ltd., 1995.

Williams, Petra. *Flow Blue China. An Aid to Identification, Volume I.* Jeffersontown, Kentucky: Fountain House East, 1971.

_____. *Flow Blue China. An Aid to Indentification, Volume II.* Jeffersontown, Kentucky: Fountain House East, 1971.

_____. *Flow Blue China. An Aid to Identification, Volume III.* Jeffersontown, Kentucky: Fountain House East, 1986.

_____. *Flow Blue China and Mulberry Ware. Similarity and Value Guide.* Jeffersontown, Kentucky: Fountain House East, 1975.

Index

Cross Reference for Terms and Trademarks

by Arnold A. Kowalsky©

back marks used for two hundred years by English potters (and others to a lesser extent by American firms) from 1780-1980. They encompass the fields of Blue & White Transferware, Historic Staffordshire, Flow Blue, Mulberry Wares, Tea Leaf/Copper Lustre Band, & White Ironstone.

There may be occasions when no mark exists at all save for the term or trade mark on the back. These marks were used to convey an image and to differentiate the potter's wares from "current" as well as other potters markings. In this way they hoped to offer something new and/or to capitalize on other potters popular sales terminologies.

Many pieces may be marked with the potters marking (either printed, impressed and/or on a pad [relief]). All marks listed may be found independently or in conjunction with known potters back stamps.

As I am researching & authorizing an encyclopedia on the foregoing, I would welcome any inquiries or additional information from collectors.

Arnold A. Kowalsky
908 North Broadway
Yonkers, NY 10701

English Marks

J. Aitchieon & Co.	-	Caledonian Pottery
Albany	-	Gibson & Sons Ltd.
Albion China		
(or Works)	-	J. Dimmock & Co.
Albion Pottery	-	Bourne & Leigh (Ltd.)
Albion Works	-	J. Dimmock & Co.
Aldwych China	-	Beswick & Son
Aldwych China	-	Bridgett & Bates
Anchor China		
(or Works)	-	Bridgwood & Son, Ltd.
Annenfield	-	John Thompson (& Sons)
Bandana	-	Charles James Mason & Co.
Barnstaple	-	C.H. Brannam Ltd.
Baxter	-	John Denton Bagster
Bedford (Ware or		
Works)	-	Ridgways (Bedford Works) Ltd.
Bellevue Pottery	-	Hull
Berlin Ironstone	-	Liddle Elliot & Son
Berlin Ironstone	-	T.J. & J. Mayer
Best	-	Livesley, Powell & Co.
Best Goods	-	Evans & Glasson
Bisto	-	Bishop & Stonier (Ltd.)
Blue Bellware	-	Longton Pottery Co. Ltd.
Blue Bellware	-	James Jamieson & Co.
Boness	-	John Marshall (& Co.) (Ltd.)
Brameld (& Co.)	-	Rockingham Pottery
Bramelds & Co.	-	Kilnhurst Old Pottery
Bridge Pottery	-	Edward F. Bodley & Son
Bristol Alkalon		
China	-	Poutney & Co. Ltd.
Bristol Porcelain	-	Poutney & Co. (Ltd.)
Bristol Pottery	-	Poutney & Goldney
Bristol Pottery	-	Poutney & Co.
Bristol Semi		
Porcelain	-	Poutney & Co. Ltd.
Britain	-	Cochran & Fleming
Britannia Pottery	-	Samuel Johnson Ltd.
British Nankin	-	Miles Mason
British Nankin China		
(or Pottery)	-	Charles James Mason & Co.
Buloch	-	David Methven & Sons
Burrleigh Ware	-	Burgess & Leigh Ltd.
Burslem (many firms		
used this mark)	-	Richard Alcock
	-	Samuel Alcock & Co.
	-	Allman, Broughton & Co.
	-	Barker & Son
	-	Barker, Sutton & Till
	-	Bodley & Co.
	-	Bridgwood & Clarke
	-	Henry Burgess
	-	Burgess & Leigh Ltd.

	-	Edward Challinor
	-	Edward Clarke & Co.
	-	Charles Collinson & Co.
	-	Cork, Edge & Malkin
	-	Edward Corn
	-	W.E. Corn
	-	Doulton & Co (Ltd.)
	-	S.W. Dean
	-	Deans (1910) Ltd.
	-	Thomas Edwards
	-	Ford & Sons (Ltd.)
	-	Samuel Ford & Co.
	-	Gibson & Sons (Ltd.)
	-	Thomas Godwin
	-	Thomas Heath
	-	Hope & Carter
	-	Hopkins & Vernon
	-	Keeling & Co. Ltd.
	-	James MacIntyre (& Co.)
	-	W.R. Midwinter (Ltd.)
	-	New Wharf Pottery Co.
	-	Newport Pottery Co. Ltd.
	-	Thos. Phillips & Son
	-	Pinder, Bourne & Co.
	-	Anthony Shaw
	-	Thomas Till & Sons
	-	John Venables & Co.
	-	Venables & Mann & Co.
	-	Wilkinson & Hulme
	-	Enoch Wood & Sons
Burslem Warranted	-	Enoch Wood & Sons
Caledonia Pottery	-	Glasgow Pottery
Calis	-	Robert Hamilton
Calyx Ware	-	Wm. Adams & Sons
Cambria	-	Charles Heathcote & Co.
Cambria	-	Swansea Pottery
Cambrian	-	Wallace & Co.
Cambrian Argil	-	Charles James Mason & Co.
Careys	-	Thomas & John Carey
Carlton China		
(or 'Ware')	-	Wiltshaw & Robinson Ltd.
Castleford (Pottery)	-	David Dunderdale & Co.
Cauldon (Ware)	-	Brown-Westhead, Moore & Co.
Cauldon Ltd.	-	Charles Allerton & Sons
Cauldon Place	-	Cauldon Ltd.
Celtic China	-	John Denton Bagster
Celtic China	-	Enoch Wood & Sons
Cetem Ware	-	C.T. Mailing & Sons (Ltd.)
Chambers, Llanelly	-	South Wales Pottery
China	-	Geo. Frederick Bowers
China	-	Hammersley & Co.
China	-	Charles Meigh & Son

China Glaze	-	Copeland & Garrett
Chinese Porcelain	-	T.J. & J. Mayer
Chinese Porcelain	-	John Rogers & Son
Chinine	-	John Tams Ltd.
City Pottery Glasgow	-	James Cooper & Sons
Cliff	-	J. Dimmock & Co.
Clyde Pottery (Co.)	-	Greenock Pottery
Coalport	-	Bradley & Co.
Cobridge	-	Henry Alcock & Co. (Ltd.)
Cobridge	-	John Alcock
Cobridge	-	John & George Alcock
Cobridge	-	Samuel Alcock
Cobridge	-	Wm. Brownfield (& Son) (s)
Cobridge	-	Furnivals Ltd.
Cobridge	-	Harding & Cockson
Cobridge	-	Meakin & Co.
Cobridge	-	Edward Pearson
Cobridge	-	Soho Pottery (Ltd.)
Cobridge	-	(R) Stevenson & Williams
Cobridge	-	Edward Walley
Cobridge	-	Wood & Brownfield
Colonial Pottery	-	F. Winkle & Co. (Ltd.)
Coombs & Holland	-	South Wales Pottery
Corona Ware	-	Gater, Hall & Co.
Cresent China	-	George Jones & Sons Ltd.
Crown Pottery	-	Ceramic Art Co. (1905) Ltd.
Crown Pottery	-	John Tams (& Son) (Ltd.)
Crown Semi Porcelain	-	J. Dimmock & Co.
Cymbro Stone China	-	Dillwyn & Co.
Cymbro Stone China	-	Swansea Pottery
Dale Hall	-	James Edwards & Son
Dale Hall Pottery	-	T.J. & J. Mayer
Deakin Pearl	-	Deakin & Co.
Denaby Pottery(ies)	-	Wilkinson & Wardle
Denby	-	Joseph Bourne & Son (Ltd.)
Derbyshire	-	Wm. Wainwright Potts
Dillwyn & Co.	-	Garrison/Sunderland Pottery
Dixon, Austin & Co. Pottery	-	Garrison/Sunderland
Dixon, Austin, Phillips & Co.	-	Garrison/Sunderland Pottery
Dixon, Phillips (& Co.)	-	Garrison/Sunderland Pottery
Don	-	Don Pottery
Don Pottery	-	Samuel Bariser & Son
Don Pottery	-	Green(s)
Dresden Opaque China	-	James & Ralph Clews
Dresden Opaque China	-	Dixon, Austin & Co.
Durability	-	J.H. Wheatherby & Sons, Ltd.
Dutchese China (The)	-	Sampson Hancock & Sons
Eastwood Works	-	J. & G. Meakin
Edinburgh	-	John Ford & Co.
Elephant Brand	-	John Tams Ltd.
Elgin Pottery -		Charles Purves
Empire Works	-	Empire Porcelain Co. (Ltd.)
Enamel Porcelain	-	Charles Meigh
Etruria	-	Davenport, Banks & Co.
Dtruria	-	Davenport, Beck & Co.
Etruria	-	Josiah Wedgwood (& Sons, Ltd.)
Etruscan Festoon	-	Wm. Ridgway & Co.
Etruscan Ware	-	Cambrian Pottery
Etruscan Ware	-	Dillwyn's
D.J. Evans & Co.	-	Swansea Pottery
Evans & Glasson	-	Swansea Pottery
Falcon Ware	-	J.H. Weatherby & Sons (Ltd.)
John Farrall	-	Pearson, Farrall & Meakin
Felspar	-	Careys
Felspar China	-	Minton
Felspar Porcelain	-	Copeland & Garrett
Felspar Porcelain	-	Minton
Fenton (used by many firms)	-	W. Barker & Co.
	-	E. & C. Challinor
	-	Challinor & Mayer
	-	James Edwards
	-	John Edwards
	-	Thomas Green
	-	E. Hughes & Co.
	-	C.J. Mason & Co.

	-	James Reeves
	-	John Yates
Fenton Potteries	-	Thomas Green
Fenton Stone Works	-	C.J. Mason & Co.
Fenton Stone Works	-	G.M. & C.J. Mason
Ferrybridge	-	Reed & Taylor
Ferrybridge	-	Sydney Woolf & Co.
Ferrybridge Pottery	-	Knottingley Pottery
Fine Stone	-	Brameld & Co.
Fleming	-	Cochran & Fleming
Flo-Blue	-	Blakeney Pottery Ltd.
Florentine China	-	Samuel Alcock & Co.
Florentine China	-	John Ridgway Bates & Co.
Foley	-	John, King, Knight
Foley Potteries	-	James F. Wileman
Foresters	-	Thomas Forester Son & Co.
Foster	-	Elsmore Forster
Fowler, Thompson & Co.	-	William Watson (& Co.)
French China	-	Hicks & Meigh
French China	-	Charles Meigh
French Porcelain	-	Samuel Alcock & Co.
Gateshead Fell	-	Sheriff Hill Pottery
Genuine Ironstone China	-	Edward F. Bodley & Co. (& Son)
Genuine Stone China	-	Stephen Foch (& Sons)
Glasgow	-	J. & M.P. Bell & Co. (Ltd.)
Glasgow	-	R. Cochran & Co.
Glasgow	-	Cochran & Fleming
Glasgow	-	John Geddes
Glasgow	-	Possil Pottery Co.
Glasgow	-	Josiah Rowley
Glasgow	-	John Thompson (& Sons)
Glasgow Pottery	-	Caledonian Pottery
Glasgow Stone China	-	Caledonian Pottery
Grafton China	-	A.B. Jones & Sons (Ltd.)
Granite	-	T. & R. Boote & Son (Ltd.)
Granite	-	Bridgwood & Clarke
Granite China (used by many firms)	-	Brameld & Co.
	-	Ferrybridge Pottery
	-	Thomas Hughes
	-	C.J. Mason & Co.
	-	Poutney & Co.
	-	Wm. Ridgway (& Co.)
	-	Ridgway & Morley
	-	Swinton Bridge
Granite Earthenware	-	T. & R. Boote & Son (Ltd.)
Granite Imperial	-	J. & M.P. Bell & Co.
Granite Opaque Pearl	-	Joseph Clementson
Granite Ware	-	Joseph Clementson
Green(s)	-	Don Pottery
George Green	-	Kilnhurst Old Pottery
Greenock Pottery	-	Clyde Pottery Co.
Gresley	-	T.G. Gren & Co. (Ltd.)
Guest & Densberry	-	South Wales Potters
Hamilton	-	Poutney & Allies
Hanley (used by many firms)	-	G.L. Ashworth & Bro.
	-	Ceramic Art Co. Ltd.
	-	Joseph Clementson
	-	Clementson Bro.
	-	J.H. & J. Davis
	-	Dudson, Wilcox & Till Ltd.
	-	Gelson Bros.
	-	Samuel Keeling & Co.
	-	Mann & Co.
	-	Charles Meakin
	-	J. & G. Meakin
	-	Charles Meigh
	-	Job Meigh (& Son)
	-	James Neal & Co.
	-	J.W. Pankhurst
	-	Wm. Ridgway Son & Co.
	-	Ridgway & Abington
	-	Ridgway & Morley
	-	William Taylor
	-	Taylor Bros.
Hartley Greens & Co.	-	Leeds Pottery
Harvey	-	Gibson & Sons Ltd.
Harvey	-	C.W.K. Harvey
Phillip Hawley & Co.	-	Kilnhurst Old Pottery
Phillip Hawley & Cook	-	Kilnhurst Old Pottery

Pattern		Maker
Thomas Hawley	-	Kilnhurst Old Pottery
William Heald	-	Kilnhurst Old Pottery
Simpson Hawley	-	Kilnhurst Old Pottery
Herculaneum	-	Job & John Jackson
Hill Pottery	-	Samuel Alcock & Co.
Hill Pottery	-	Burgess & Leigh (Ltd.)
Hill Works	-	Barker & Son
Holkirkware	-	Hollinshead & Kirkham (Ltd.)
Wm. Holland	-	South Wales Pottery
W.T. Holland	-	Ynsonedw Pottery
Holland & Guest	-	South Wales Pottery
Hull	-	Belle Vue Pottery
Hylton Pot Works	-	Maling
Hylton Pot Works	-	John Phillips
Hylton Pottery	-	John Phillips
Imperial	-	Wm. Adams & Sons (Ltd.)
Imperial	-	J. & M.P. Bell & Co.
Imperial China	-	Enoch Wood & Sons
Imperial French Porcelain	-	Wm. Adams
Imperial Granite	-	Podmore Walker & Co.
Imperial Ironstone	-	Morley & Ashworth
Imperial Ironstone China (used by many firms)	-	Henry Alcock
	-	John Alcock
	-	Samuel Alcock & Co.
	-	(W.) Baker & Co.
	-	Baker & Chetwynd & Co.
	-	Birks Bros. & Seddon
	-	Robert Cochran & Co.
	-	Cockson & Chetwynd
	-	C. Collinson & Co.
	-	W. & E. Corn
	-	Hollinshead & Kirkham
	-	St. Johns Chinaware Co.
	-	Podmore, Walker & Co.
	-	Wedgwood & Co. Ltd.
Imperial Parisian Granite	-	Old Hall Earthenware Co.
Imperial Porcelain	-	Wedgwood & Co. (Ltd.)
Imperial Semi China	-	Charles Allerton & Sons
Imperial Semi Porcelain	-	Myott Son & Co. (Ltd.)
Imperial Stone	-	J. & G. Alcock
Imperial Stone	-	John Ridgway (& Co.)
Imperial Stone	-	Wm. Ridgway Son & Co.
Imperial Stone	-	Ridgway & Abington
Imperial Stone	-	Ralph Stevenson & Sons
Imperial Stone China	-	Charles Meigh
Imperial Stone China	-	John Ridgway & Co.
Imperial Stone China	-	Ralph Stevenson & Son
Imperial White Granite	-	Pinder, Bourne & Co.
Imperial Wreath	-	Cockson & Harding
Improved Berlin Ironstone	-	T.J. & J. Mayer
Improved China	-	Job Meigh (& Son)
Improved China	-	Wm. Ridgway (& Co.)
Improved Granite China	-	Ridgway & Morley
Improved Granite China	-	Ridgway, Morley, Wear & Co.
Improved Granite China	-	Wm. Ridgway (& Co.)
Improved Ironstone	-	Wm. Adams
Improved Ironstone	-	Charles Meigh
Improved Ironstone China	-	Charles James Mason & Co.
Improved Ironstone China	-	T.J. & J. Mayer
Improved Ironstone China	-	Charles Meigh (& Son)
Improved Ironstone China Stoke Works	-	Stephen Foch (& Sons)
Improved Saxon Blue	-	Dillwyn & Co.
Improved Stone	-	Wm. Ridgway & Co.
Improved Stone China (used by many firms)	-	Cochran & Co.
	-	Hicks & Meigh
	-	Thomas Mayer
	-	Charles Meigh (& Son)

Pattern		Maker
Improved Stoneware	-	Job Meigh (& Son)
Improved Stoneware	-	Minton
Indian Ironstone	-	Minton & Boyle
Indian Ironstone	-	Poutney & Allies
Indian Stone	-	Dillwyn & Co.
Indian Stone	-	Thos. Dimmock
Indian Stone China	-	John & George Alcock
Indian Stone China	-	Samuel Alcock & Co.
Indian Stone China	-	John & George Alcock
	-	Edward Walley
	-	Hicks & Meigh
	-	Charles Meigh & Son
	-	Old Hall Earthenware Co. Ltd.
Ironstone (used by many firms)	-	Wm. Adams (& Sons)
	-	Henry Alcock
	-	G.L. Ashworth Bros.
	-	Bishop & Stonier
	-	T. & R. Boote
	-	Booth & Meigh
	-	Joseph Bourne
	-	Geo. Frederick Bowers & Co.
	-	Brougham & Mayer
	-	Ed. Challinor
	-	Ed. Challinor & Co.
	-	Joseph Clementson
	-	Clementson, Young & Anderson
	-	Cork, Edge & Malkin
	-	John Cormi
	-	John Davenport
	-	Davenport Ltd.
	-	Edge, Malkin & Co.
	-	James Edwards
	-	John Edwards
	-	James & Thomas Edwards
	-	Jacob Furnival & Co.
	-	Thos. Furnival (& Co) (& Sons)
	-	Thomas Godwin
	-	Thomas Goodfellow
	-	Joseph Goodin
	-	John Goodwin (& Co.)
	-	Hollinshead & Kirkham
	-	Lively, Powell & Co.
	-	Mason (& partnerships)
	-	T.J. & J. Mayer
	-	Mayer & Elliot
	-	Meakin & Co.
	-	Charles Meigh
	-	John Meir (& Son)(s)
	-	Mellor, Venables & Co.
	-	Frances Morley (& Co.)
	-	George Phillips & Son
	-	Podmore, Walker & Co.
	-	Powell & Bishop
	-	Anthony Shaw
	-	South Wales Potters
	-	Thomas Till & Son
	-	Thomas Walker
	-	John Wedg.Wood
	-	W. Williams
	-	Wood & Challinor
	-	Geo. Wooliscroft
	-	Ynsonedw Pottery
Ironstone China (used by many firms)	-	Wm. Adams
	-	Ashworth's (Bros.)
	-	(W.) Barker & Co.
	-	Samuel Barker & Son
	-	Barrow & Co.
	-	Bishop & Stonier
	-	Joseph Bourne (& Son) (Ltd.)
	-	G.F. Bowers & Co.
	-	Henry Burgess
	-	Samuel & John Burton
	-	Dunn Bennett & Co. (Ltd.)
	-	E. & C. Challinor
	-	John Cormie
	-	James Edwards (& Son)
	-	James & Thomas Edwards
	-	John Edwards
	-	Thomas Goodfellow
	-	Hackwood
	-	Thomas Hughes
	-	Livesley, Powell & Co.

Term		Trademark
	-	John Maddox (& Sons) (Ltd.)
	-	G.M. & C.J. Mason
	-	Henry Meakin
	-	J. & G. Meakin
	-	Meakin & Co.
	-	Pearson, Farrall & Meakin
	-	Powell & Bishop
	-	Ridgways (Bedford Wks) Ltd.
	-	St. John Stone Chinaware Co.
	-	South Wales Potters
	-	Edward Walley
	-	James F. Wileman
	-	Arthur Wilkinson, Ltd.
	-	Wood & Son(s) Ltd.
Ironstone China Stoke Works	-	Stephen Folch (& Sons)
Ironstone China Warranted	-	Anthony Shaw
Ironstone Ware	-	Thomas Hughes & Son (Ltd.)
Ironstone Ware Ltd.	-	Ridgways (Bedford Wks)
Ivory China	-	Ridgways (Bedford Wks) Ltd.
Ivory Ware	-	Clementson Bros.
Janroth	-	Ridgways (Bedford Wks) Ltd.
Kaolin (Ware)	-	Thomas Dimmock (Jr.) & Co.
Kaolin (Ware)	-	F. & R. Pratt
Kemp & Co.	-	Caledonian Pottery
Kilnhurst Old Pottery	-	Geo. Green
Kirkcaldy Pottery	-	David Methuen & Co.
Knottingley Pottery	-	Ferrybridge Pottery
Landore Pottery	-	John F. Calland & Co.
Lane Delph	-	C.J. Mason & Co.
Lane End	-	Booth & Meigh
Lane End	-	Thomas Harley
Lane End	-	Thomas Walley
Lasol (Ware)	-	Keeling & Co. Ltd.
Late W. Adams & Sons	-	Close & Co.
Late R. Alcock	-	A.J. Wilkinson
Late Hackwood	-	Cockson & Harding
Late Harvey	-	Holland & Green
Late Mayers	-	Samuel Keeling & Co.
Late Spode	-	W.T. Copeland (& Sons Ltd.)
Late Spode	-	Copeland & Garrett
Late Wedgwood	-	Hollinshead & Kirkham (Ltd.)
Lawleys Ltd.	-	Hollinshead & Kirkham (Ltd.)
Leeds	-	Pettys & Co.
Leeds Pottery	-	Hartley Greens & Co.
Limited	-	Davenport Ltd.
Limoge P.G.	-	Sampson Bridgwood & Son (Ltd.)
Lincoln Pottery	-	Samuel Ford & Co.
Liverpool	-	John Goodwin & Co.
Liverpool	-	Herculaneum Pottery
Llanelly	-	South Wales Potteries
London	-	Malkin, Walker & Hulse
London	-	Middlesbrough Pottery
Longport (used by many firms)	-	Edward Clarke & Co.
	-	W. & E. Corn
	-	Wm. Davenport (& Co.) (Ltd.)
	-	John & Joseph Mayer
	-	Thomas Mayer
	-	T. & J. Mayer
	-	T.J. & J. Mayer
	-	Edward & George Phillips
	-	George Phillips
	-	Thomas Phillips & Son
	-	Joseph Stubbs
	-	Stubbs & Kent
	-	Arthur Wood & Sons Ltd.
Longton (used by many firms)	-	Baggerley & Ball
	-	Barker Bros. (Ltd.)
	-	William Bourne
	-	Colclough & Co.
	-	Davenport & Co.
	-	John Goodwin
	-	Hammersley & Co.
	-	Hammersley & Asbury
	-	John Thomas Hudden
	-	Frederick Jones (& Co.)
	-	James Kent
	-	Longton Pottery Co.
	-	John Tams
Low Ford	-	Dawson (John Dawson & Co.)
Low Lights Pottery	-	John Carr (& Co.)(& Son(s))
Lowndes & Beech	-	Beech & Lowndes
Lustrosa	-	G.L. Ashworth & Bros. (Ltd.)
M./Stone	-	Minton
Made In Scotland	-	Cochran & Fleming
William Malpass	-	Kilnhurst Old Pottery
Mandarin Opaque China	-	Poutney & Goldney
Manufactured to the King	-	Brameld & Co.
Mason's	-	G.L. Ashworth & Bros. (Ltd.)
Mason's	-	Charles James Mason (& Co.)
Mason's	-	G.M. & C.J. Mason
Mason's Ironstone	-	Francis Morley (& Co.)
Micratex	-	Wm. Adams & Son Ltd.
Middlesbrough	-	Isaac Wilson & Co.
Middleport Potters (Pottery)	-	Burgess & Leigh (Ltd.)
Andrew Muir & Co.	-	Clyde Pottery
Murray & Co.	-	Caledonian Pottery
Muse	-	William Reid, Scotland
Donald McLaughlin & Brown(ie)	-	Clyde Pottery
Nankin Ware	-	John Tams Ltd.
Nautilus Porcelain	-	Nautilus Porcelain Co.
Nautilus Porcelain	-	Possil Pottery Co.
Newbiggins Pottery	-	Wm. Reid (& Sons)
Newbiggins Pottery	-	Wm. Reid & Forster
Newbridge Pottery	-	Edward F. Bodley & Son
New Canton	-	Andrew Stevenson
New Castle	-	Thomas Fell & Co.
New Castle	-	John Wood & Co. (Ltd.)
New Castle	-	John Wood & Co.
New Castle on Tyne	-	C.T. Maling & Sons (Ltd.)
New Castle Upon Tyne	-	Bell, Cook & Co.
New Fayence	-	Josiah Spode
New Hill	-	Joseph Twigg (Bros.) (& Co.)
New Japan Stone	-	Copeland & Garrett
New Stone	-	S. Keeling & Co.
New Stone	-	Josiah Spode
New Stone China	-	C.J. Mason & Co.
New Stone China	-	Ralph Stevenson & Son
New Wharf	-	Thomas Godwin
New Wharf(e)	-	Thomas & Benjamin Godwin
Norfolk Pottery Stone	-	Lawleys Ltd.
North British Pottery	-	Alexander Balfour
Northshields	-	John Carr & Sons
Northumberland	-	John Carr (& Co.)(& Son(s))
Old English Bone China	-	Allertons Ltd.
Old Hall	-	Job Meigh (& Sons)
Old Hall	-	Old Hall Earthenware Co. Ltd.
Old Hall	-	Old Hall Porcelain Works Ltd
Opaque China (used by many firms)	-	Baggerley & Ball
	-	Baker, Bevans & Irwin
	-	Belle Vue Pottery
	-	T. & R. Boote & Son (Ltd.)
	-	Bourne, Baker & Bourne
	-	Bridgwood & Clarke
	-	Davenport (et al.)
	-	James Edwards
	-	Elkin, Knight & Bridgwood
	-	Elkin, Knight & Co.
	-	Elsmore & Forster
	-	Goodwin(s) & Harris
	-	George Gordon
	-	Sampson Hancock & Sons
	-	C. & W.K. Harvey
	-	Lockett & Hulme
	-	Mayer & Newbold
	-	Charles Meigh (& Son)
	-	Minton
	-	Francis Morley (& Co.)
	-	Edward & George Phillips
	-	George Phillips
	-	Reed & Taylor
	-	John Ridgway (& Co.)
	-	John & William Ridgway
	-	Wm. Ridgway (& Co.)
	-	Ridgway & Morley
	-	Ridgway, Morley & Wear & Co.
	-	Ridgways

	-	John & Richard Riley	
		Wood & Challinor	
Opaque China			Pearl White Ironstone	-	Cork & Edge
Warranted	-	Jacob Marsh	Pearl White Ironstone	-	South Wales Pottery
Opaque Felspar			Phillips & Co.	-	Garrison Pottery
China	-	Elkin & Knight/Knight, Elkin & Co.	Phillips & Co.	-	Sunderland Pottery
Opaque Granite	-	Wm. Ridgway (& Co.)	J.Phillips	-	Garrison Pottery
Opaque Granite			J. Phillips	-	Sunderland Pottery
China	-	Australian Pottery	Phoenix China		
Opaque Granite			(Ware)	-	Thomas Forrester & Sons Ltd.
China	-	Ferrybridge Pottery	Porcelain	-	James Edwards
Opaque Granite			Porcelain A La		
China	-	John, King, Knight	Francaise	-	John Ridgway & Co.
Opaque Granite			Porcelain A La Perle	-	James & Thomas Edwards
China	-	Wm. Ridgway (& Co.)	Opaque Porcelain		
Opaque Pearl	-	Joseph Clementson	(used by many firms)	-	Sampson Bridgwood & Son
Opaque Porcelain	-	Bridgwood & Clarke		-	Bridgwood & Clarke
Opaque Porcelain	-	C. & W.K. Harvey		-	John Carr & Son
Opaque Porcelain	-	Charles Meigh & Son		-	Cochran & Fleming
Opaque Porcelain	-	Old Hall Earthenware Co. Ltd.		-	James & Thomas Edwards
Opaque Stone	-	John & Geo. Alcock		-	Thomas Edwards
Opaque Stone	-	John & Samuel Alcock		-	Thomas Fell & Co.
Opaque Stone China	-	Robinson, Wood & Brownfield		-	James Jamleson & Co.
Opaque Stone China	-	Anthony Shaw & Son(s) (& Co.)		-	Charles Meigh
Oriental Ivory	-	Powell, Biship & Stonier		-	David Methven & Sons
Oriental Stone	-	John Alcock		-	Anthony Shaw (& Son(s)) (& Co.)
Oriental Stone	-	John & George Alcock	Porcelain Royale	-	Cleveland Pottery
Ortolan	-	Deakin & Son(s)	Porcelain Royale	-	Pitcairns Ltd.
Palissy	-	Albert E. Jones (Longton) Ltd.	Porcelaine De Terre	-	John Edwards (& Co.)
Palissy	-	Palissy Pottery Ltd.	Porcelaine Royale		
Paris White	-	Edward Walley	(Artware)	-	W. & E. Corn
Parisian Granite	-	T.G. & F. Booth	Porcelon	-	W.R. Midwinter Ltd.
Parisian Granite	-	Sampson Bridgwood & Son (Ltd.)	Potters to Her		
Parisian Granite	-	Elsmore & Son	Majesty	-	Cauldon Ltd.
Patent	-	Samuel Alcock & Co.	Pottery	-	G.R. Turnbull
Patent	-	Ford & Challinor	Pouls On Brothers	-	Ferrybridge Pottery
Patent	-	Francis Morley (& Co.)	Prestopans	-	Belfield & Co.
Patent	-	Machin & Potts	Published By	-	Wm. Ridgway Son & Co.
Patent	-	Ridgway & Morley	Charles Purves	-	Elgin Pottery
Patent	-	Wm. Wainwright Potts	Quartz China	-	Wm. Ridgway (& Co.)
Patent	-	Enoch Wood & Sons	Queens Ware/		
Patent Ironstone			Stockton	-	Skinner & Walker
China (used by			Queens Ware/		
many firms)	-	G.L. Ashworth & Bros.	Stockton	-	Wm. Smith & Co.
	-	Wm. Davenport	Real English		
	-	F. Jones & Co.	Ironstone	-	Wm. Adams & Sons
	-	James Mason	Real Ironstone	-	H. & R. Daniel
	-	C.J. Mason & Co.	Real Ironstone	-	James Edwards (& Son)
	-	C.M. & C.J. Mason	Real Ironstone	-	Thomas Furnival & Co.
	-	Frances Morley & Co.	Real Ironstone		
	-	Morley & Ashworth	Chine (used by many		
	-	Ridgway & Morley	firms)	-	Wm. Adams & Sons
	-	Josiah Spode		-	G.L. Ashworth & Bros. (Ltd.)
	-	John Turner		-	John Davenport
	-	Turner & Co.		-	Davenport Ltd.
Patent Mosaic	-	Cork & Edge		-	James Edwards (& Son)
Patent Opaque China	-	Francis Morley & Co.		-	Jacob Furnival & Co.
Patent Paris White				-	C. & W.K. Harvey
Ironstone	-	Wedgwood & Co. Ltd.		-	Holland & Green
Patent Staffordshire	-	James & Ralph Clews		-	Alfred Meakin Ltd.
Pearl	-	Cockson & Chetwynd		-	Mellor, Taylor & Co.
Pearl	-	Charles Collinson & Co.		-	Francis Morley (& Co.)
Pearl	-	Deakin & Co.		-	Morley & Ashworth
Pearl	-	Peter Holdcroft & Co.		-	John Ridgway (& Co.)
Pearl	-	Podmore, Walker & Co.		-	John & William Ridgway
Pearl	-	Tomkinson Bros. & Co.		-	Wm. Ridgway
Pearl	-	Josiah Wedgwood (& Sons, Ltd.)		-	Ridgway & Morley
Pearl China	-	(W.) Baker & Co. Ltd.		-	Ridgway, Morley, Wear & Co.
Pearl China	-	Samuel & John Burton	Real Stone China	-	Ashworth's (Bros.)
Pearl China	-	J. & G. Meakin (Ltd.)	Real Stone China	-	Davenport Ltd.
Pearl China	-	Enoch & Edward Wood	Real Stone China	-	Hicks, Meigh & Johnson
Pearl Ironstone China	-	Ford, Challinor & Co.	Real Stone China	-	Francis Morley & Co.
Pearl Ironstone China	-	Frederick Jones & Co.	Reed & Taylor	-	Ferrybridge Pottery
Pearl Ironstone China	-	George Phillips	Reid & Patterson	-	Caledonian Pottery
Pearl Ironstone China	-	Turner & Tomkinson	Rock Stone	-	John Tams
Pearl Stone China	-	Podmore, Walker & Co.	Rockingham Works	-	Brameld & Co.
Pearl Stoneware	-	Podmore, Walker & Co.	Romantic	-	Blakeney Pottery Ltd.
Pearl Ware	-	Samuel Alcock & Co.	Romantic	-	Cartwright & Edwards Ltd.
Pearl Ware	-	Thomas Dimmock	Joseph Rawley	-	Caledonian Pottery
Pearl Ware	-	Skinner & Walker	Royal	-	J. & M.P. Bell & Co.
Pearl White	-	(W.) Baker & Co. Ltd.	Royal Art Pottery	-	Alfred Clough Ltd.
Pearl White	-	Edward Walley	Royal Art Pottery	-	Cloughs Royal Art Pottery
Pearl White	-	Wood & Brownfield	Royal China	-	E. Hughes & Co.
Pearl White Granite	-	(W.) Baker & Co. (Ltd.)	Royal Coronation		
			Ware	-	Sampson Hancock & Sons
			Royal Crownford		

Term		Firm
Ironstone	-	J.H. Weatherby & Sons Ltd.
Royal Ironstone		
China (used by		
many firms)	-	Henry Alcock & Co.
	-	Baker & Co., Ltd.
	-	T. & R. Boote
	-	Caledonian Pottery
	-	Cochran & Fleming
	-	W. & E. Corn
	-	Deans (1910) Ltd.
	-	W.H. Grindley & Co. (Ltd.)
	-	Johnson Bros. (Hanley) Ltd.
	-	Alfred Meakin (Ltd.)
	-	Melor, Taylor & Co.
	-	Arthur J. Wilkinson (Ltd.)
Royal Ironstone Ware	-	Johnson Bros. (Hanley) Ltd.
Royal Ivory	-	John Maddock & Sons Ltd.
Royal Patent	-	T. & R. Boote Ltd.
Royal Patent	-	Clementson Bros.
Royal Patent		
Ironstone	-	T. & R. Boote Ltd.
Royal Patent		
Ironstone	-	Thos. Hughes & Son
Royal Patent		
Ironstone	-	Turner, Goddard & Co.
Royal Patent		
Stoneware	-	Clementson Bros.
Royal Premium Semi		
Porcelain	-	T. & R. Boote Ltd.
Royal Rockingham		
Works	-	Brameld & Co.
Royal Semi China	-	James Kent (Ltd.)
Royal Semi Porcelain		
(used by many firms)	-	T. & R. Boote Ltd.
	-	Booths (Ltd.)
	-	Bourne & Leigh (Ltd.)
	-	Burgess & Leigh
	-	Edward Clarke & Co.
	-	Clementson Bros.
	-	Alfred Colley & Co. Ltd.
	-	Furnivals Ltd.
	-	Johnson Bros (Hanley) Ltd.
	-	John Maddock & Sons (Ltd.)
	-	Alfred Meakin Ltd.
	-	Ridgways
	-	Arthur J. Wilkinson (Ltd.)
	-	Wood & Son(s) (Ltd.)
Royal Staffordshire	-	Arthur J. Wilkinson (Ltd.)
Royal Stanley (Ware)	-	Colclough & Co.
Royal Stanley (Ware)	-	Stanley Pottery Ltd.
Royal Stone China	-	Ashworth Bros.
Royal Stone China	-	J. & M.P Bell & Co.
Royal Stone China	-	H.H. & J. Davis
Royal Stone China	-	John Maddock & Sons Ltd.
Royal Stone China	-	Francis Morley (& Co.)
Royal Stone China	-	Ralph Stevenson & William
Royal Stone China	-	Wedgwood & Co.
Royal Vitreous	-	John Maddock & Sons (Ltd.)
Royal Vitrescent Rock		
China	-	Machin & Potts
Royal Vitrified	-	John Maddock & Sons (Ltd.)
Royal Vitrified	-	Ridgways
Saxon	-	Clyde Pottery Co.
Saxon	-	Thomas Shirley & Co.
Saxon Blue	-	Dillwyn & co.
Saxon China	-	James Edwards
Saxon Stone China	-	Thomas & John Carey
Scotia Pottery	-	Edward F. Bodley & Son
Scotia Pottery	-	Bodley & Harold
Scott (Bros.)(& Co.)		
(& Sons)	-	Southwick Pottery
Scotland	-	David Methven & Sons
Scott Bros.	-	Edinburg Scotland
Seacombe Pottery	-	John Goodwin
Seacombe Pottery	-	Goodwin & Co.
Seaham Pottery	-	John Allason
Semi China (used by		
many firms)	-	Henry Alcock & Co. Ltd.
	-	Clementson Bros.
	-	Elgin Pottery
	-	Thomas & Benjamin Goodwin
	-	John & Richard Riley
	-	John Rogers & Son
	-	Tams & Co.

Term		Firm
	-	Fowler Thompson & Co.
	-	James Wallace & Co.
	-	Enoch Wood & Sons
Semi China Warranted	-	C.J. Mason & Co.
Semi China Warranted	-	G.M. & C.J. Mason
Semi China Warranted	-	John & Richard Riley
Semi China Warranted	-	Ralph Stevenson
Semi Nanking China	-	Andrew Stevenson
Semi Porcelain (used		
by many firms)	-	(The) Henry Alcock & Co. Pottery
	-	T. & R. Boote (Ltd.)
	-	Bridgwood & Son Ltd.
	-	Burgess & Leigh
	-	Samuel Ford & Co.
	-	Globe Pottery Co.
	-	Grimwades Ltd.
	-	J. & G. Meakin (Ltd.)
	-	Mellor, Taylor & Co.
	-	Myott, Son & Co.
	-	New Wharf Pottery Co.
	-	Poutney & Co.
	-	Ridgways (Bedford Wks) Ltd.
	-	Soho Pottery Ltd.
Semi Royal Porcelain	-	Josiah Wedgwood & Sons Ltd.
Semi Royal Porcelain	-	Wedgwood & Co. (Ltd.)
Sevres	-	James & Thomas Edwards
Sewells	-	Sewell & Co.
Sharpus	-	London Retailers
Shelton	-	Joseph Clementson
Shelton	-	Francis Morley (& Co.)
Shelton	-	Wm. Ridgway & Co.
Shelton	-	Ridgways (Bedford Wks)
Sheriff Hill Pottery	-	Ford & Patterson (& Co.)
Thomas Shirley & Co.	-	Clyde Pottery
Silicon China	-	Booths (Ltd.)
Silicon China	-	Dillwyn & Co.
Silicon China	-	James Edwards
Simpson-Bowman		
Heald	-	Kilnhurst Old Pottery
Sol	-	J. & G. Meakin (Ltd.)
Solian Ware	-	Soho Pottery Ltd.
South Hylton	-	Dawson (John Dawson & Co.)
South Wales Pottery	-	Guest & Densberry
Southwick	-	Southwick Pottery
Special White Stone		
Ware	-	Clementson Bros. Ltd.
Spodes Imperial	-	Copeland & Garrett
St. Rollox	-	Robert Cochran & Co.
Stafford Pottery	-	William Smith & Co.
Staffordshire (used by		
many firms)	-	John Denton Bagster
	-	(W.) Baker & Co.
	-	Batkin, Walker & Broadhurst
	-	Booths (Ltd.)
	-	William Bourne & Co.
	-	John Brindley & Co.
	-	Ceramic Art Co. (Ltd.)
	-	Edward Challinor
	-	J. T. Close & Co.
	-	Cork & Edge
	-	W. & E. Corn
	-	Thomas Edwards
	-	Godwin, Rowley & Co.
	-	Thomas Mayer
	-	Myott, Son & Co.
	-	Andrew Stevenson
	-	Ralph Stevenson
	-	R. Stevenson & William
	-	Edward Walley
	-	Enoch Wood & Sons Staffordshire Ironstone
China	-	Griffiths, Beardmore & Birks
Staffordshire Ironstone		
China	-	George Townsend
Staffordshire Potteries	-	C.J. Mason & Co.
Staffordshire Stone		
China	-	Godwin, Rowley & Co.
Staffordshire Stone		
Ware	-	Cork & Edge
Staffordshire		
Warranted	-	Andrew Stevenson
Stanley China	-	Charles Amison (& Co.Ltd.)
Stanley Pottery	-	Colclough & Co.
Stepney (Pottery)	-	G.R. Turnbull
Stepney (Pottery)	-	John Wood & Co. (Ltd.)

James Stevenson & Co. - Clyde Pottery
Stockton - Skinner & Walker
Stockton - W. Smith & Co.
Stockton - John & Wm. Ridgway
Stoke - Robert Hamilton
Stoke - Thomas Mayer
Stoke - T.J. & J. Mayer
Stoke - George Thomas Mountford
Stoke - Myott, Son & Co.
Stoke - F. Winkle & Co. Ltd.
Stoke - Woolfe & Hamilton
Stone China - W. Baker & Co.
Stone China - Baker & Till
Stone China - James & Ralph Clews
Stone China - Thomas Godwin
Stone China - Josiah Wedgwood (& Sons)(Ltd.)
Stoke on Trent (used by many firms) - Ceramic Art Co. (1905) Ltd.
- J.T. Close & Co.
- Colclough & Co.
- Empire Porcelain Co. (Ltd.)
- Grimwades Ltd.
- Hammersley & Co.
- Geo. Jones (& Sons Ltd.)
- Stanley Pottery Ltd.
Stoke Manufacturers - Zacharia Boyle (& Co.)(& Son(s))
Stoke On Trent - Empire Porcelain Co. (Ltd.)
Stoke On Trent - Grimwades Ltd.
Stoke Pottery - J. Plant & Co.
Stoke Upon Trent - J.T. Close & Co.
Stoke Upon Trent - Grimwade Bros.
Stoke Upon Trent - Thomas Mayer
Stoke Upon Trent - Minton
Stoke Upon Trent - Ridgways (Bedford Wks) Ltd.
Stoke Works - Stephen Foch (& Sons)
Stone - Charles Meigh
Stone - Minton
Stone China (used by many firms) -
- Wm. Adams & Sons
- Wm. Baker & Co. Ltd.
- Barker, Sutton & Till
- Barker & Till
- Brameld & Co.
- Batkin, Walker & Broadhurst
- Caledonian Pottery
- Edward Clarke (& Co.)
- Joseph Clementson
- Clementson Bros.
- James & Ralph Clews
- J.T. Close & Co.
- R. Cochran & Co.
- Cork & Edge
- Cork, Edge & Malkin
- H. & R. Daniel
- Davenport (& Co)(Ltd.)
- Wm. Davenport (Ltd.)
- James Edwards (& Son)
- Jacob & Thomas Furnival
- Thomas Godwin
- Thomas & Benjamin Godwin
- Godwin, Rowley & Co.
- Ralph Hall
- Hicks & Meigh
- Hicks, Meigh & Johnson
- Hope & Carter
- Geo. Jones (& Sons Ltd.)
- John Maddock (& Sons (Ltd.)
- Maddock & Seddon
- John Meir & Son
- Minton
- J.W. Pankhurst & Co.
- Plymouth Pottery Co. Ltd.
- James Reed
- Reed & Taylor & Co.
- John & William Ridgway
- Robinson & Wood
- Robinson, Wood & Brownfield
- Rowley & Co.
- Anthony Shaw
- Josiah Spode
- Stafford Pottery
- Ralph Stevenson & William
- William Taylor
- Joseph Twigg (& Bro.) (& Co.)
- Edward Walley
- Josiah Wedgwood (& Sons Ltd.)
- Wedgwood & co.
- Wedgwood's (J. Wedgwood & Sons)
- Whitehaven Pottery

- Wood & Brownfield
- Wood & Challinor
Stone Chinaware Co. - St. Johns Stoneware Co. (Canada)
Stone Ware (used by many firms) -
- Samuel Alcock & Co.
- Wm. Barker & Son
- Barker, Sutton & Till
- Barker & Till
- Joseph Burn & Co.
- Joseph Clementson
- Clementson Bros.
- C.J.T. Close & Co.
- H. & R. Daniel
- Wm. Davenport (& Co.)
- Thomas Dimmock (& Co.)
- J. Maudesley & Co.
- T.J. & J. Mayer
- Francis Morley
- Podmore, Walker & Co.
- Read & Co.
- Read & Clementson
- James Reed
- Ridgway & Morley
- Robinson, Wood & Brownfield
- John Thompson
- Thomas Till & Son(s)
- Wedgwood & Co. (Ltd.)
Sunderland - (Samuel) Moore & Co.
Sunderland - John Phillips
Sunderland Pottery - J. Phillips
Sundrex - Sunderland Pottery Co. (Ltd.)
Superior Staffordshire Ware - Jones & Son
Superior Stone China - John Ridgway (& Co.)
Sutherland Art Ware - Frank Beardmore & Co.
Swadlincote - Thomas Sharpe
Swansea - T.J. Bevington & Co.
Swansea - John F. Calland & Co.
Swansea - Cambrian Pottery
Swansea - Dillwyn & Co.
Swansea - D.J. Evans & Co.
Swansea - Evans & Glasson
Sytch Pottery - Thomas Till & Sons
John Tams (& Sons) (Ltd.) - Crown Pottery
Tomlinson & Co. - Ferrybridge Pottery
Tomlinson & Co. - Knottingley Pottery
Trade Mark - Green & Clay
Trade Mark - W.H. Grindley & Co. (Ltd.)
Tunstall (used by many firms) -
- Wm. Adams
- W. & T. Adams
- T.G. & F. Booth
- G.F. Bowers & Co.
- Edward Challinor
- Edward Clarke & Co.
- Alfred Colley & Co. Ltd.
- Cumberlidge & Humphreys
- Elsmore & Forster
- Joseph Goodwin
- W.H. Grindley & Co. (Ltd.)
- Hollinshead & Kirkham (Ltd.)
- Humphreys Bros.
- Alfred Meakin
- John Meir & Son
- Pitcairns Ltd.
- Soho Pottery
- E.T. Troutbeck
- G.W. Turner & Sons
- Thomas Walker
Turner & Co. - Kilnhurst Old Pottery
Turner & Phillip
Hawley
Turner & Thomas - Kilnhurst Old Pottery
Hawley
Turners - Kilnhurst Old Pottery
Tuscan China - G.W. Turner & Sons
Benjamin & John - R.H. & S.L. Plant (Ltd.)
Twigg
Daniel Twigg - Kilnhurst Old Pottery
John Twigg - Kilnhurst Old Pottery
Tyne - John Wood & Co. (Ltd.)
Tyne Pottery - Patterson & Co.
Tynside - Bell, Cook & Co.
Vedgwood - Carr & Patton
Vedgwood - Wm. Smith (& Co.)
Verreville Glasgow - John Geddes
Victoria - Blakeney Pottery Ltd.
Victoria - Cartwright & Edwards Ltd.

Victoria China	-	James Reeves
Vine	-	J. & M.P. Bell & Co.
Viterous Ironstone	-	Dunn, Bennett & Co. (Ltd.)
Vitrified	-	John Maddock & Sons Ltd.
Warranted (used by many firms)	-	
	-	Batkin, Walker & Broadhurst
	-	T. & R. Boote
	-	Joseph Bourne (& Sons Ltd.)
	-	John Brimdley & Co.
	-	Edward Challinor
	-	Chesworth & Robinson
	-	Chetham & Robinson
	-	Joseph Clementson
	-	James & Ralph Clews
	-	Clyde Pottery Co.
	-	Dale, Deakin & Bayley
	-	James Edwards
	-	John Edwards
	-	Job & John Jackson
	-	Charles James Mason & Co.
	-	John Meir & Son(s)
	-	John & Richard Riley
	-	Anthony Shaw (& Son(s)) (& Co.)
	-	Thomas Shirley & Co.
	-	Stafford Pottery
	-	Andrew Stevenson
	-	Ralph Stevenson
	-	Enoch Wood & Sons
	-	Yale & Barker
Warranted English Stone China	-	Challinor & Mayer
Warranted Ironstone China	-	Baggerley & Ball
Warranted Ironstone China	-	Batkin, Walker & Broadhurst
Warranted Ironstone China	-	James & Ralph Clews
Warranted Ironstone China	-	John Edwards (& Co.)
Warranted Staffordshire	-	John Brindley & Co.
Warranted Staffordshire	-	John Carr & Son
Warranted Staffordshire	-	James & Ralph Clews
Warranted Staffordshire	-	John Meir (& Sons)
Warranted Staffordshire	-	S. Tams & Co.
Warranted Stone China	-	Joseph Clementson
Warranted Stone China	-	James & Ralph Clews
Warranted Stone China	-	Mellor, Taylor & Co.
Warranted Stone China	-	Whitehaven Pottery
Warranted/Stone China/Fenton	-	John Yates
Waterloo Potteries	-	T. & R. Boote (Ltd.)
Wm. Watson & Co.	-	Fowler Thompson (& Co.)
Wedg-Wood	-	John Wedg.Wood
Wedgewood	-	Wm. Smith (& Co.)
Wedgwood	-	Podmore, Wakler & Co.
Wedgwood	-	Josiah Wedgwood (& Sons Ltd.)
Wedgwood	-	Ralph Wedgwood
Wedgwood & Co.	-	Ferrybridge Pottery
Wedgwood & Co.	-	Knottingley Pottery
Wedgwood & Co.	-	Podmore, Walker & Co.
Wedgwood & Co.	-	Ralph Wedgwood & Co.
Wedgwood & Co.	-	Wedgwood & Co. (Ltd.)
Wedgwood Place/Burslem	-	Allman, Broughton & Co.
Wedgwood Ware	-	Wm. Smith (& Co.)
Wharf	-	Thomas Godwin
White Enamel China	-	Enoch Wood
White Granite	-	Cork, Edge & Malkin
White Granite	-	Anthony Shaw (& Son) (& Co.)
White Granite Ironstone	-	Bishop & Stonier (Ltd.)
Whitehaven	-	Whitehaven Pottery
Whittington Moor	-	Pearson & Co.
Wilkinson (John)		
Pottery	-	Whitehaven Pottery
Williams Williams	-	Ynysmedw Pottery
Wood	-	Enoch Wood
Edmunt T. Wood	-	John (Wedg) Wood
Woodland (Pottery)	-	Hollinshead & Kirkham Ltd.
Wood North & Co.	-	Whitehaven Pottery
Woods	-	Wood & Sons Ltd.
Lewis Woofl (& Sons)	-	Ferrybridge Pottery
Ye Old Foley Ware	-	James Kent Ltd.
American Marks		
Adamantine China	-	Wheeling Pottery Co.
Alpaugh & Magowan	-	Empire Pottery Co.
Alpaugh & Magowan	-	Trenton Potteries
American Pottery Co.	-	Jersey City Pottery
American Pottery Manufacturing Co.	-	Jersey City Pottery
American Pottery Works	-	Sebring Pottery (Works) Co.
Avon Works	-	Vance Faience
Bloor, Ott & Booth	-	Etruria Pottery Co.
William Brunt	-	Dresden Pottery Co.
William Brunt	-	Great Western Pottery
William Brunt	-	Phoenix Pottery
William Brunt	-	Riverside Knob Works
Burgess & Campbell	-	International Pottery Co./Lincoln Pottery Co.
Burgess & Co.	-	International Pottery Co./Lincoln Pottery Co.
James Carr & Edward Clark	-	International Pottery Co./Lincoln Pottery Co.
Carr & Morrison	-	McNichol-Burton Pottery Co.
James Carr	-	New York City Pottery
Cook & Hancock	-	Crescent Pottery Co.
Coxon & Co.	-	Empire Pottery Co.
Crescent Pottery Co.	-	Trenton Potteries Co.
Dale & Davis	-	Prospect Hill Pottery
Isaac Davis	-	Prospect Hill
Isaac Davis	-	Trenton Pottery Co.
Delaware Pottery Co.	-	Trenton Potteries Co.
Dresden Pottery Works	-	Potters Co-operative & Dresden Pottery Co.
Eagle Pottery	-	Burroughs & Mountford
Eagle Pottery Co.	-	J.M. Forrest & Co.
East Liverpool Potteries	-	United States Pottery Co.
Empire Pottery Co.	-	Trenton Pottery Co.
Enterprise Pottery Co.	-	Trenton Potteries Co.
Equitable Pottery Co.	-	Trenton Potteries Co.
Etruria Pottery Co.	-	Cook Pottery
Fredericksburg	-	American Beleek
Great Western Pottery (Co.)	-	John Wyllie & Son
D.F. Haynes & Co.	-	Chesapeake Pottery (& Co.)
Ideal Pottery	-	Trenton Potteries Co.
International Pottery Co.	-	Burgess & Campbell
LaBelle China	-	Wheeling Pottery Co.
Lamberton China	-	Maddock Pottery Co.
Lamberton China	-	Sterling China Co.
Manley & Cartwright	-	Cartwright Bros.
Mellor & Co.	-	Cook (& Mellor) Pottery Co.
John Moses & Sons Co.	-	Glasgow Pottery
Novelty Pottery Co.	-	McNichol-Burton Pottery Co.
Ott & Brewer (Bloor)	-	Etruria Pottery
Phoenix Pottery	-	Phoenixville Pottery Co.
Phoenix Pottery	-	Schreiber & Betz
Phoenix Pottery	-	Beerbower & Griffen
Pioneer Pottery Works	-	(Gates, p. 211 & Lehner, p. 349)
Red Cliff	-	Hall China Co.
Red Cliff	-	Walker Co.
Riverside Pottery	-	Wheeling Pottery Co.
Royal Blue	-	Burgess & Campbell
Schreiber & Betz	-	Phoenixville Pottery
Henry Speeler (& Sons)	-	International Pottery Co.
Sterling China Co.	-	Limoges China Co.
Syracuse Pottery (China) Co.	-	Onondaga
Taylor & Co (& various partnerships)	-	Trenton Potteries
Trenton Pottery	-	Prospect Hill Pottery
Trenton Pottery	-	Fell & Thropp
Vance Faience Co.	-	Wheeling Pottery Co.
Wellesville Pioneer (China) & Pottery Co.	-	Pioneer Pottery Co. (Gates p. 309 & Lehner p. 510)
Wood & Barlow	-	Empire Pottery

Index of Patterns

On pages 166 through 168 is an index of patterns found in all five of my books on this subject: Flow Blue (1992, revised 1996 & 1998), Historic Flow Blue (1994), A Pocket Guide to Flow Blue (1995), Fascinating Flow Blue (1997), and Flow Blue: A Closer Look (2000). This should provide a useful cross-reference when you are searching for one special pattern and its value.

Pattern Names	Flow Blue	Historic Flow Blue	Pocket Guide to Flow Blue	Fascinating Flow Blue	Flow Blue: A Closer Look
Abbey	16, 26, 75-76				
Acadia		74			
Acme			36		
Adderley		132			
Adelaide		132			
Alaska	76	56			161
Albany	76-77				111, 162
Aldine					111
Alma		29	52		
Althea				10	
Amherst Japan		133	107		
Amoy	30	5, 10, 15, 16, 18, 75-76	9, 34, 60	25, 34, 36, 38, 48, 59, 73, 81-82	
Anemone		62			
Apples					112
Arabesque	16, 30	30, 59	19, 61	37, 59, 82-83	
Arcadia	78-79			33	165
Argyle	79	133	44, 109		112, 142, 160, 167
Arvista	79				
"Asiatic Birds"				73	
Asiatic Pheasant	80				
"Astor & Grape Shot"				83	
Astoria					112, 167
Atalanta	80				
Athens	31			84	
Athol	80-81				
Atlas		133			
Aubrey	22, 25, 81-82				
Avon		133			
Ayr	82	26			
Babes in the Woods					168
Balmoral	83				
Bamboo		7, 35, 52, 76-77	62	84	
Basket			42	35, 42	
Basket Pattern No. 204				74	
Beaufort	83				113
Beauties of China	9, 31		63	5, 12	
Bell	84				
Bentick	84				140, 166
Benton	155				
Berry		77			
Bimrah		78	63		
Blackberry		78-79		50, 60, 85	
"Bleeding Heart"				33, 69	
Blenhiem	26, 84-85				
Blossom			110		142
Blue Bell		13, 17, 32, 79-80, 122-123	12, 95	30, 35, 85-86	
Blue Bell & Grapes w/ Cherry Border				86	
Blue Danube	85	26			162
Blue Onion					168
Blue Rose		7			
Brazil		134	111		113
Briar					114, 168
Brooklyn					162
Brunswick	85				
Brush stroke				4, 24-25, 35-36, 56, 60, 71, 74, 76	
Burleigh		40, 134			164
Byronia			41	87	
Cabul		36, 80	64	87-88	
Calico					140, 142
California		64			
Cambridge	85-86				163, 166
Candia	86			89	143
Canton	32	54			

Pattern Names	Flow Blue	Historic Flow Blue	Pocket Guide to Flow Blue	Fascinating Flow Blue	Flow Blue: A Closer Look
Canton Vine				90	
Carlsbad	86				
Carlton		80		33, 93	
Cashmere	33, 34	16	45, 64	17, 40, 45, 62, 66, 90-93	
Cavendish					169-170
Cecil		134			163
Celtic					114, 159
Ceylon	61				
Chapoo	24, 34, 35	6	7, 9, 39, 65	15, 65, 93-95	5, 12, 37-47
Chen Si	36		13, 66	35, 75	
Chelsea		135			
Chiang	36				
Chinese	37	81	20, 47	20, 23, 27, 95-96	
Chineses Bells		33			
Chinese Dragons		5			
Chinese Landscape		36, 44, 124-125	96	140	
Chinese Musicians				13	
Chinese Pagoda		32	53		
Chinese Sports				75	
Ching		82			
Chrysanthemum				35	
Chusan		5, 9, 25, 27-28, 49, 82-83, 135-136	30, 36, 45, 51, 67-68, 113	28, 30, 34, 47, 54, 97-100	
Circassia	36				
Ciris				28	
Claremont					170
Clarence	87				114, 167, 171
Claremont Groups				136	
Clayton	87-89				161
Clifton	90				160
Clyde					155
Clytie					171-172
Coburg	61-62		58	52-53, 55, 65, 100-102	155
Colonial	90				115
Columbia	21, 37				
Convulvulus				103	
Conway	91-92				
Corey Hill					172
Corinthian Flute	92				
Countess					159, 166
Cows					172
Cracked Ice					115, 140, 143
Croxton	93				
Crumlin		137			163, 165
Cypress	93	12	69		
Dahlia		83	70		
Dainty	94				164
Daisy					173
Daisy Chain					142
Damask Rose		125	97		
Davenport	94				
Dejapore		84			
Delamere	94				
Delft					116, 143
Delph	95-96			141	165
Derby		27			
Deva		138			
Devon		46			163
Dog-Rose					173
Doreen					11
Doric					174
Doris	96	22			
Dorothy	10, 97-98				
Dovedale					116
Drayton					174-175
Dresden	98				
Dresden Flowers					143

Pattern Names	Flow Blue	Historic Flow Blue	Pocket Guide to Flow Blue	Fascinating Flow Blue	Flow Blue: A Closer Look
Pansy					140-141, 147, 179
Peach		155			127, 162
Pekin	6, 49, 128	19, 156			
Peking	49	107-109		120-121	
Pelew	6, 50		82	29, 36, 121	
Penang				120	
Peony					179
Persian					162
Persian Moss	128-129				
Persian Spray	129-130			155	127-129
Persiana		24, 129	94	139	
Perth	6, 130				
Petunia					180
Pheasant	51				
"Pinwheel"		109		20	
Plymouth		45			
"Pomegranate"		156			
Poppy	131		54		130, 180
Portman		156-157			131, 160
Princeton	132				161
Progress					131
Prunus					148
Reeds & Flowers				15	148
Regal	132-133	158			
Regina	133				
Renown		158			
Rhine		112			
Rhoda Gardens		112			
Rhone	51	112-113		68, 122	
Rialto	133				
Richmond	133-134	27			
Rock	51				
Roma					163
Rose	134	158			
Rose & Jasmine		113			
Roseville		27, 158			
Roxbury		159			
Royal Blue		67-68	135		
Royston		159			
Ruby					148
Ruins		159			
Savoy	134-135				164
Scinde	52-55	18, 29, 43, 114-116	28-29, 83-88	6, 14, 32-33, 37, 42-43, 52, 72, 79, 122-127	79, 127
"Scott's Bar"					127
Scroll				127	
Seaweed					131, 181
Senator	135				
Servants					158
Shanghae	71	27	99	26, 53, 67	
Shanghai	72			6	
Shapoo	55		89		
Shell		4, 38, 129-130	100-102	32, 140	
Siam		159	33		
Simla		130	103		
Singa	56	31	48	140	
Sloe Blossom		31	48	35	158-159
"Snowflake"				80	
Snowflower		160-161	136		
Sobraon	56	116	90	51, 128	
Sphinx		38			
"Spinach"		162			
St. Louis					131, 161, 165
Stanley	138				161
"Stratford"		162			
"Strawberry"		29	104	49, 129	
Swiss	72				
Switzerland					132
Sydenham	72				
Sylvan					132
Syrian					181
Talli		162			
Tedworth		163			
Temple	56	116		46, 48, 59	
Tivoli	57	11		61	
Togo		163			
Tonquin	57-58	27, 119	8, 20, 44, 91-92	37, 67, 129-131	
Touraine	138-140	6	137	38, 155-156	4, 102-110
"Tree of Life"		119			
Trent			138		
Trilby	77, 140				
Troy	58	61		69	
"Tulip"		118			
"Tulip & Fern"		117		104, 132	
"Tulip & Sprig"		117		57, 61-62, 132	
Turkey					182-183
Tuscon			33		
Venice	142				
Vermont	143-145				
Verona	146				139, 163
Versailles					164
Victoria	146	20			
Vienna					165
Vine Border		120			
Waldorf	146-147			157	
Warwick				68, 133	139, 162, 184
Washington Vase	60				
Water Nymph	73				
Watteau	147		32, 139-141		15, 154
Waverly					161
Whampoa			93	37, 134-135	
Wheel	153				
Wild Rose					140-141, 155, 185
Willow		131, 166-168	57, 142-143		155, 167
Windsor Scrolls				35, 40	
Yellow River				135	